Jesus Knows- Our Hearts, Our Responsibility

Joshua Rhoades

Published by Joshua Paul Rhoades, 2024.

JESUS KNOWS- OUR HEARTS, OUR RESPONSIBILITY

First edition. August 31, 2024.

Copyright © 2024 Joshua Rhoades.

ISBN: 979-8227510112

Written by Joshua Rhoades.

Also by Joshua Rhoades

Courage Under Fire: David's Stand On The Battlefield
Jonah's Journey: Voices Of Redemption And Lessons In Obedience
The Furnace Of Faith: 12 Principles From The Heat Of Faith
Whispers of Hope: Inspiring Stories of Men's Prayers In Scripture
Frontier Legends: The Oregon Dream
Elijah: A Beacon Of Boldness
HOOK, LINE & SAVIOUR - Faith Reflections from Fishing
Driven By Faith: Motor Racing Inspired Christian Life
30 Day Devotional - Bold and Strong- Coffee Devotions for a
Courageous Christian Walk
Authentic Christianity: The Heart of Old Time Religion
Consider The Ant - God's Tiny Preachers
Flee Fornication: The Plea For Purity
Renewed Hope- How to Find Encouragement in God
Sounding The Call - The Voice of Conviction
The Altar - Where Heaven Meets Earth
The Bible's Battlefields- Timeless Lessons from Ancient Wars
The Sacred Art of Silence - How Silence Speaks in Scripture
Under Fire- The Sanctity of the Traditional Biblical Home
Who Is on the Lord's Side? A Call to Righteousness
What Is Truth? - From Skepticism to Submission
First and Goal- Faith and Football Fundamentals
From Dugout to Devotion- Spiritual Lessons from Baseball
Par for the Course- Faith and Fairways
The Believer's Pace- Tools for Running Life's Marathon

Introduction

"Jesus Knows: Our Hearts, Our Responsibility" dives into the profound truth that Jesus, in His infinite wisdom and love, knows us more deeply than we know ourselves. The Bible, repeatedly affirms that God is intimately acquainted with every detail of our lives—our thoughts, desires, struggles, and intentions. In Psalm 139:1-2, we are reminded, "O LORD, thou hast searched me, and known me. Thou knowest my downsitting and mine uprising, thou understandest my thought afar off." This scripture underscores the inescapable reality that nothing about us is hidden from Jesus. He sees beyond our outward actions and appearances, right into the very core of our being—our hearts.

This book invites you to explore the implications of this divine knowledge. If Jesus knows our hearts, what does that mean for how we live? What responsibilities does this knowledge place upon us? Far from being a passive observation, Jesus' awareness of our innermost thoughts and feelings calls us to a higher standard of living—a life marked by integrity, accountability, and a deep commitment to aligning our hearts with His will. The knowledge that Jesus sees everything about us should not evoke fear or shame, but rather inspire us to live more authentically and purposefully.

In a world that often encourages superficiality and pretense, the truth that Jesus knows our hearts is both a challenge and a comfort. It challenges us because it means we can't hide our true selves from Him. We are called to examine our motives, confess our sins, and strive to live lives that are pleasing to God—not just in our actions, but in the intentions behind those actions. Jesus' knowledge of our hearts means we are responsible for what we allow to dwell there—whether it's love, faith, and purity, or bitterness, pride, and deceit.

However, this truth also brings great comfort. Knowing that Jesus understands our hearts means He sees our struggles, our pain, and our sincere efforts to follow Him, even when we fall short. He knows the desires we have to do good, even when we fail, and He offers grace and strength to help us grow. This intimate knowledge is a testament to His deep love for us—a love that invites us to come to Him with all our burdens, confident that He will help us carry them.

"Jesus Knows: Our Hearts, Our Responsibility" is an invitation to live with a greater awareness of God's presence in our lives. It challenges us to take responsibility for our inner lives, knowing that what we nurture in our hearts will ultimately shape our actions and our character. As you read through these pages, may you be encouraged to cultivate a heart that is fully devoted to God, embracing the responsibility that comes with being known by Jesus and responding to His knowledge with a life of genuine faith, integrity, and love.

Chapter 1 - Your Soul

"But Jesus did not commit himself unto them, because he knew all men, And needed not that any should testify of man: for he knew what was in man." (John 2:24-25)

This passage highlights how Jesus, being the Son of God, possesses a profound and complete knowledge of every person. He understands our hearts, minds, and souls in ways that no one else can. When it says Jesus "knew all men," it means He understands the essence of who we are—our innermost thoughts, feelings, and motivations. He doesn't need anyone to inform Him about us because His knowledge is already perfect and all-encompassing.

Our soul is the core of our being, the part of us that transcends physical existence. It includes our mind, will, and emotions—everything that makes us unique individuals. Jesus knows our soul completely. This deep understanding means He is aware of our deepest desires, fears, and joys. Even the thoughts and feelings we might not share with others are fully known to Him. For instance, when we experience happiness, sadness, or anxiety, Jesus understands these emotions intimately. He recognizes the sources of our feelings and offers comfort and guidance through them.

Moreover, Jesus's knowledge of our soul includes an awareness of our needs. Before we even articulate our needs in prayer, He already knows what we require for our well-being. This divine insight assures us that we are never alone in our struggles. Jesus's knowledge is not just intellectual; it is also empathetic. He feels our pain and rejoices in our successes. His empathy is rooted in His own experiences as a human being who faced challenges, temptations, and suffering.

Jesus's awareness of our sins is another significant aspect of His knowledge. He sees the wrong choices we make, even those we try to hide. Yet, His response is not one of condemnation but of forgiveness. He offers us the chance to repent and start anew. This aspect of His knowledge highlights His unconditional love and mercy. Knowing that we are fully seen, including our flaws and mistakes, and still loved deeply by Jesus can be a source of great comfort and encouragement.

Understanding Jesus's knowledge of our soul also involves recognizing that He is aware of our potential and purpose. He knows the gifts and talents we possess and the unique path we are meant to follow. This divine insight helps guide us toward fulfilling our God-given purpose. When we seek His guidance, we can trust that He will lead us in the right direction, helping us to grow and develop in ways that align with His will for our lives.

Furthermore, Jesus's comprehensive knowledge extends to our relationships and interactions with others. He understands the dynamics of our connections with family, friends, and even strangers. He sees the love, support, and sometimes the conflicts and misunderstandings that arise. By knowing these aspects of our lives, Jesus can provide wisdom and guidance on how to navigate and nurture our relationships.

In times of trial and suffering, the knowledge that Jesus fully understands our soul can be incredibly reassuring. He is aware of the burdens we carry and the struggles we face. His understanding presence offers us strength and hope, reminding us that we are not alone. His empathy and compassion provide comfort and encouragement, helping us to persevere through difficult times.

Jesus's knowledge of our soul also includes an understanding of our spiritual journey. He sees our faith, our doubts, and our spiritual growth. He knows the efforts we make to live according to His teachings and the times we fall short. His awareness of our spiritual state allows Him to provide the support and guidance we need to deepen our relationship with Him and grow in our faith.

Moreover, Jesus's knowledge of our soul highlights His role as our intercessor. He advocates for us before God the Father, understanding our needs and concerns better than anyone else. This advocacy is rooted in His intimate knowledge of our hearts and souls, ensuring that our prayers and petitions are presented with perfect understanding and love.

The awareness that Jesus knows our soul completely can inspire us to live authentically and honestly. Since nothing about us is hidden from Him, we can be open and transparent in our relationship with Him. This authenticity allows us to experience a deeper connection with Jesus, one that is based on genuine love and trust.

Additionally, Jesus's knowledge of our soul emphasizes the importance of personal integrity and accountability. Knowing that He sees and understands our innermost thoughts and actions encourages us to live with integrity, making choices that reflect our faith and values. This awareness fosters a sense of accountability, motivating us to strive for righteousness and holiness in our daily lives.

Understanding that Jesus knows our soul completely also enhances our sense of self-worth and identity. We are fully known and fully loved by the Creator of the universe. This profound truth affirms our inherent value and worth, reminding us that we are cherished and significant in the eyes of God. This understanding can boost our self-esteem and help us navigate life's challenges with confidence and assurance.

Furthermore, Jesus's knowledge of our soul underscores His role as our shepherd and guide. Just as a shepherd knows each sheep intimately, Jesus knows each of us personally. He leads us with wisdom and care, guiding us along the paths that are best for us. His knowledge ensures that He can provide the right direction, protection, and provision at every step of our journey.

In conclusion, the Lord's complete knowledge of our soul, as described in John 2:24-25, is a testament to His divine wisdom, love, and compassion. Jesus's intimate understanding of our innermost being assures us that we are never alone and that we are deeply valued and loved. This knowledge provides comfort, guidance, and encouragement, helping us to live authentically, grow spiritually, and fulfill our God-given purpose. Embracing this truth can transform our lives, fostering a deeper relationship with Jesus and a greater sense of peace, hope, and joy in our daily walk with Him.

Chapter 2 - Your Speculations

"But Jesus, knowing their thoughts, said, Wherefore think ye evil in your hearts?" (Matthew 9:4)

This verse highlights the fact that Jesus, who is the Son of God, possesses an incredible ability to know all our thoughts and speculations. Speculations are the things we think about, question, and wonder about in our minds. They include our doubts, fears, dreams, plans, and even the things we might not want to admit to ourselves. Jesus knows all of these, which means He understands us better than anyone else ever could. He doesn't need us to tell Him what we are thinking because He already knows. This deep understanding of our thoughts is part of His divine nature.

When we think about how Jesus knows our speculations, it means He is aware of every idea that crosses our mind. Whether these thoughts are good or bad, positive or negative, Jesus sees them all. This can be both comforting and a bit intimidating. On one hand, it is reassuring to know that someone understands us completely, even the parts of ourselves that we might struggle to understand. On the other hand, it reminds us that we are never truly alone in our thoughts. Jesus knows when we are happy, when we are sad, and when we are confused. He knows our hopes and dreams, our fears and doubts.

This knowledge that Jesus has about our speculations is not just surface-level. He understands the reasons behind our thoughts. For example, if we are worried about something, He knows why we are worried. If we are excited about a new opportunity, He understands why we feel that way. His understanding is complete and perfect. This means that Jesus can offer us exactly the support and guidance we need, tailored to our unique situation and mindset. When we pray and talk to Jesus, we can be confident that He already knows what is on our mind and what we need help with.

Furthermore, knowing that Jesus understands our speculations means He is aware of the times we struggle with negative thoughts. When we think poorly of ourselves or others, He sees these thoughts. The verse from Matthew 9:4 specifically mentions Jesus addressing evil thoughts in the hearts of the people He was speaking to. This shows that He is aware of the moral quality of our thoughts and can guide us to better thinking. Jesus does not condemn us for our thoughts, but He calls us to recognize and change them if they are harmful or wrong. His knowledge of our speculations includes a deep compassion and desire to help us grow.

Jesus's awareness of our thoughts also includes the positive and constructive speculations we have. When we plan to do something good, like helping a friend or working hard in school, He knows these intentions and supports us. He encourages us to think positively and to make plans that align with His teachings and values. This means that we can turn to Jesus for inspiration and motivation when we need it. He understands our goals and aspirations and wants to help us achieve them in a way that is good for us and others.

Additionally, Jesus knowing our speculations means that He is aware of the times we question or doubt. Everyone has moments of doubt or confusion, whether it is about faith, life choices, or other important matters. Jesus sees these doubts and does not judge us for them. Instead, He offers us patience and understanding. He wants to help us find answers and clarity. This can be incredibly comforting because it means we don't have to hide our uncertainties from Him. We can be honest about our struggles and seek His guidance and reassurance.

When we understand that Jesus knows all our speculations, it can change the way we think and live. Knowing that He sees and understands our every thought can encourage us to be more mindful and intentional with our thinking. It can inspire us to cultivate positive and constructive thoughts, to seek His guidance in times of confusion, and to trust that He is with us in all our mental and emotional journeys. Jesus's knowledge of our speculations is a reminder of His deep and abiding presence in our lives.

This deep understanding of our thoughts also means that Jesus is aware of our intellectual pursuits and curiosities. He knows when we are trying to learn new things or solve problems. He sees our efforts to understand the world and our place in it. This knowledge means that He is a source of wisdom and insight. When we are curious or seeking knowledge, we can turn to Him for guidance and understanding. He encourages us to explore and learn, knowing that our intellectual growth is an important part of who we are.

Moreover, Jesus's understanding of our speculations means that He is aware of our internal conflicts and struggles. Everyone experiences times when they feel conflicted or torn between different choices or feelings. Jesus sees these internal battles and offers His support. He understands the complexity of our emotions and thoughts and can help us navigate through them. This means that in times of internal struggle, we can find peace and clarity in Jesus's presence and guidance.

Jesus's knowledge of our speculations also includes an awareness of our spiritual thoughts and questions. He sees when we ponder over spiritual matters, when we seek to understand our faith more deeply, and when we have questions about God and His teachings. This means that Jesus is always ready to help us in our spiritual journey. He understands our need for spiritual growth and offers His wisdom and support. We can turn to Him with our spiritual questions and trust that He will guide us to the answers we seek.

Furthermore, knowing that Jesus understands our speculations can provide a sense of accountability. Since He is aware of our thoughts, we might feel encouraged to keep our minds focused on positive and righteous things. This awareness can motivate us to avoid negative or harmful thinking and instead cultivate thoughts that are in line with

His teachings. It can inspire us to be more mindful of our mental habits and strive to think in ways that are pleasing to Him.

In conclusion, understanding that the Lord knows all our speculations, as described in Matthew 9:4, is a profound realization that can deeply impact our lives. Jesus's complete knowledge of our thoughts means that He understands us better than anyone else. He sees our deepest desires, fears, and dreams. He knows our needs and offers the perfect support and guidance. His awareness of our negative thoughts includes a compassionate call to change and grow. He understands our positive intentions and supports our good plans. His knowledge of our doubts and questions means that He offers patience and clarity. Jesus's understanding extends to our intellectual pursuits, internal conflicts, and spiritual questions. This deep and comprehensive knowledge provides comfort, guidance, and encouragement. It can inspire us to be more mindful and intentional with our thinking, to seek His guidance, and to trust in His presence. Knowing that Jesus sees and understands all our speculations reminds us of His deep and abiding love for us. It encourages us to live with integrity, to cultivate positive thoughts, and to seek His wisdom in all areas of our lives. Jesus's knowledge of our speculations is a testament to His divine wisdom and compassion, offering us support and guidance in our mental and emotional journeys. Embracing this truth can transform our lives, fostering a deeper relationship with Jesus and a greater sense of peace, hope, and joy in our daily walk with Him. This profound understanding can boost our self-esteem and help us navigate life's challenges with confidence and assurance. It is a source of great comfort and strength, guiding us through the ups and downs of life and helping us to become the best versions of ourselves.

Chapter 3 - Your Sustenance

"Be not ye therefore like unto them: for your Father knoweth what things ye have need of, before ye ask him." (Matthew 6:8)

This verse highlights the amazing truth that God, our Father, knows exactly what we need even before we ask Him. Sustenance refers to everything we need to survive and thrive, including food, water, shelter, love, and spiritual nourishment. Jesus, being the Son of God, is fully aware of all these needs and provides for us in ways we might not even realize. This complete understanding and provision are part of His divine nature.

Jesus knowing our sustenance means He is aware of our physical needs, like food and water. He knows when we are hungry or thirsty and ensures that we have what we need to stay healthy and strong. In the Bible, there are many instances where Jesus provided for people's physical needs, like when He fed the five thousand with just five loaves of bread and two fish. This miracle shows His power and His deep care for our well-being. He knows when we are in need and is always ready to provide for us.

But Jesus's knowledge of our needs goes beyond just physical sustenance. He also understands our emotional needs. He knows when we need love, comfort, and support. Life can be challenging, and we all face times of sadness, stress, and loneliness. During these times, Jesus is there to offer His love and comfort. He understands what we are going through and provides the emotional support we need to keep going. His love is unconditional, and He is always there for us, ready to lift us up when we are feeling down.

Jesus also knows our need for spiritual sustenance. Just as our bodies need food and water, our souls need spiritual nourishment to stay healthy and strong. Jesus provides this through His teachings, His presence, and His love. Spending time in prayer, reading the Bible, and being part of a faith community are ways we can receive this spiritual sustenance. Jesus knows that our souls need to be fed with His word and His love, and He provides us with the guidance and support we need to grow spiritually. He wants us to have a close relationship with Him, and He offers everything we need to make that possible.

In addition to understanding our individual needs, Jesus also knows the needs of our families and communities. He sees the struggles we face in our relationships and provides guidance and support to help us navigate these challenges. Whether it's a family going through a tough time or a community facing hardship, Jesus is aware of these needs and works through people and situations to provide help and support. His knowledge of our needs is complete, and His provision is perfect.

Jesus's understanding of our needs also means He is aware of our future needs. He knows what lies ahead and prepares us for the challenges and opportunities we will face. This foresight is part of His divine wisdom. We might not know what the future holds, but Jesus does, and He ensures that we are equipped with everything we need to handle whatever comes our way. This can be a great source of comfort and confidence, knowing that we are never alone and that Jesus is always looking out for us.

Another important aspect of Jesus knowing our sustenance is His awareness of our need for purpose and fulfillment. He knows that we all have a desire to live meaningful lives and to use our talents and abilities to make a difference in the world. Jesus provides us with opportunities to fulfill this need by guiding us towards our unique purpose and calling. He knows our strengths and weaknesses and helps us to use them in ways that bring joy and fulfillment. His guidance ensures that we can live lives that are not only satisfying to us but also glorify Him and help others.

Jesus's knowledge of our sustenance also includes our need for rest and relaxation. In our busy and often stressful lives, it's easy to forget the importance of rest. But Jesus knows that we need time to recharge and refresh. He encourages us to take time for rest, to spend time in His presence, and to find peace in Him. He knows that rest is essential for our physical, emotional, and spiritual well-being. By following His example and taking time for rest, we can stay healthy and strong in all areas of our lives.

Understanding that Jesus knows all our needs can change the way we approach life. It can help us to trust Him more and to rely on His provision. When we worry about our needs, whether they are physical, emotional, or spiritual, we can remember that Jesus already knows what we need and is ready to provide for us. This trust can bring a sense of peace and security, knowing that we are in His care. We can be confident that Jesus will provide for us, even in times of difficulty and uncertainty.

Moreover, knowing that Jesus understands our needs can inspire us to be more aware of the needs of others. Just as He provides for us, we can be His hands and feet in the world, helping to provide for the needs of those around us. This can include offering physical help, emotional support, or spiritual encouragement. By following Jesus's example, we can make a positive difference in the lives of others and help to build a caring and supportive community.

Jesus's knowledge of our sustenance also highlights the importance of gratitude. When we recognize that He provides for all our needs, it can lead us to be more thankful for His blessings. Practicing gratitude can enhance our relationship with Jesus and help us to see His hand at work in our lives. It can also bring joy and contentment, knowing that we are cared for and loved by our Savior. Taking time to thank Jesus for His provision can deepen our faith and strengthen our trust in Him.

In conclusion, understanding that the Lord knows all about our sustenance, as described in Matthew 6:8, is a profound and comforting truth. Jesus's complete knowledge of our needs means that He understands and provides for every aspect of our well-being, including our physical, emotional, and spiritual needs. His awareness of our future needs ensures that we are prepared for whatever lies ahead. His understanding of our need for purpose and fulfillment guides us towards meaningful lives. His recognition of our need for rest reminds us to take time to recharge. This comprehensive knowledge of our sustenance can transform our lives, bringing us peace, trust, and gratitude. It can inspire us to be more aware of the needs of others and to offer help and support in His name. Embracing this truth can deepen our relationship with Jesus and bring us closer to Him, fostering a sense of security and confidence in His provision. Jesus's knowledge of our sustenance is a testament to His divine wisdom, love, and compassion, providing us with everything we need to live fulfilling and purposeful lives.

Chapter 4 – Your Sins

"And Jesus knowing their thoughts said, Wherefore think ye evil in your hearts?" (Matthew 9:4)

This verse shows that Jesus, who is the Son of God, has the incredible ability to know all our thoughts, including the evil or sinful ones. Jesus doesn't need anyone to tell Him about our sins because He already knows them. This deep understanding is part of His divine nature. Knowing our sins means that Jesus is aware of every wrong thing we do, every mistake we make, and every evil thought we have. Even when we try to hide our sins from others, we cannot hide them from Jesus. He sees everything clearly. This knowledge can be both comforting and challenging. On one hand, it means that we are fully known by Jesus. He sees our true selves, including our flaws and imperfections. On the other hand, it reminds us that we are accountable for our actions and thoughts. We cannot hide anything from Jesus. He sees the good and the bad, and He knows our hearts.

Jesus knowing our sins means He is aware of the times we fail to live up to His teachings. Sin is anything that goes against God's will and separates us from Him. It can be actions, thoughts, or attitudes that are harmful to ourselves or others. Jesus sees these sins and understands their impact on our lives. He knows how sin can hurt us and those around us. His knowledge of our sins is not just about judgment, but also about His deep desire to help us overcome them. Jesus wants us to recognize our sins, repent, and seek forgiveness. His awareness of our sins comes from a place of love and compassion. He knows that sin can lead us away from Him, and He wants to bring us back into a close relationship with Him.

One of the most comforting aspects of Jesus knowing our sins is His offer of forgiveness. Even though He sees all our wrongdoings, He does not turn away from us. Instead, He invites us to confess our sins and receive His forgiveness. The Bible tells us that if we confess our sins, Jesus is faithful and just to forgive us and cleanse us from all unrighteousness. This promise of forgiveness is a testament to His immense love and grace. Jesus understands that we are not perfect and that we will make mistakes. His knowledge of our sins is accompanied by His willingness to forgive and help us start anew. This forgiveness is not something we earn; it is a gift from Jesus. Knowing this can bring us great comfort and peace.

Understanding that Jesus knows our sins also means He is aware of the times we struggle with guilt and shame. When we sin, we often feel guilty and ashamed. These feelings can weigh heavily on us and make us feel unworthy of God's love. Jesus sees our guilt and shame and offers us His healing and grace. He knows that carrying the burden of sin can be difficult, and He invites us to lay our burdens at His feet. Jesus's knowledge of our sins is accompanied by His deep compassion. He wants us to experience freedom from guilt and shame through His forgiveness. By accepting His forgiveness, we can let go of the past and move forward with a clean slate.

Jesus's understanding of our sins also means that He knows our weaknesses and temptations. He sees the areas where we are most likely to fall into sin and understands the struggles we face. This knowledge allows Him to offer us the support and strength we need to resist temptation and make better choices. Jesus does not leave us to fight our battles alone. He is with us, offering His guidance and help. By relying on His strength, we can overcome our weaknesses and grow in our faith. Jesus's awareness of our sins and weaknesses is not meant to condemn us, but to help us become the people He created us to be. He knows our potential and wants to help us live up to it.

Another important aspect of Jesus knowing our sins is His call to repentance. Repentance means turning away from sin and turning towards God. It involves acknowledging our sins, feeling remorse, and making a commitment to change. Jesus's knowledge of our sins is a call to repentance. He wants us to recognize the ways we have strayed from

His path and make a conscious effort to return to Him. Repentance is not just about saying sorry; it is about making a real change in our lives. Jesus offers us the opportunity to repent and be transformed by His love and grace. This transformation is a process that requires effort and dedication, but Jesus is with us every step of the way, guiding and supporting us.

Jesus's knowledge of our sins also means that He is aware of the ways we try to justify or hide our wrongdoings. Sometimes, we might try to make excuses for our sins or pretend they are not that bad. Jesus sees through these justifications and understands the true nature of our actions. He calls us to be honest with ourselves and with Him. Hiding or justifying our sins only keeps us trapped in them. By being honest about our sins, we can receive Jesus's forgiveness and begin the process of healing and growth. Jesus's knowledge of our sins is a reminder that we cannot hide anything from Him. He sees everything clearly and calls us to live in the light of His truth.

Understanding that Jesus knows our sins can also help us to be more compassionate and forgiving towards others. Just as we are aware of our own sins and need for forgiveness, we can recognize that others are in the same situation. Everyone makes mistakes and needs grace. By understanding this, we can be more patient and forgiving with those around us. Jesus's knowledge of our sins teaches us the importance of forgiveness and compassion. He forgives us and calls us to forgive others. This can create a cycle of grace and love in our relationships, helping us to build stronger and more loving communities.

In conclusion, understanding that the Lord knows all about our sins, as described in Matthew 9:4, is a profound and transformative truth. Jesus's complete knowledge of our sins means that He sees and understands every wrong thing we do, every mistake we make, and every evil thought we have. His knowledge is not just about judgment, but about His deep desire to help us overcome sin and live in a close relationship with Him. Jesus's awareness of our sins is accompanied by

His offer of forgiveness, His compassion for our guilt and shame, His support in our weaknesses, His call to repentance, and His guidance towards honesty and transformation. This comprehensive understanding of our sins can bring us great comfort and peace, knowing that we are fully known and fully loved by Jesus. It can inspire us to seek His forgiveness, to repent and make positive changes in our lives, and to be more compassionate and forgiving towards others. Embracing this truth can deepen our relationship with Jesus and bring us closer to Him, fostering a sense of security and confidence in His love and grace. Jesus's knowledge of our sins is a testament to His divine wisdom, love, and compassion, offering us the opportunity for healing, growth, and transformation. This understanding can change our lives, helping us to live in the light of His truth and love, and to become the people He created us to be.

Chapter 5 - Your Sorrows

"He is despised and rejected of men; a man of sorrows, and acquainted with grief..." (Isaiah 53:3)

This verse refers to Jesus, who is known as a man of sorrows and is familiar with suffering and grief. Jesus, the Son of God, experienced rejection, pain, and sadness during His time on Earth. Because of this, He deeply understands our own sorrows and grief. This means that Jesus knows every sad moment we experience, every disappointment, every heartbreak, and every loss. He is not distant or unaware of our pain; He is intimately familiar with it. This knowledge is part of His divine nature and shows His deep compassion and love for us.

When we talk about Jesus knowing our sorrows, it means He is aware of every instance of pain and sadness in our lives. Whether it is a small disappointment or a major tragedy, Jesus knows what we are going through. He understands the sadness of losing a loved one, the pain of a broken relationship, the fear of an uncertain future, and the struggle of dealing with illness or hardship. His own experiences with sorrow and rejection give Him a unique perspective on our suffering. He knows what it feels like to be rejected and despised, to feel lonely and misunderstood. This deep understanding means that Jesus is not only aware of our sorrows but also empathizes with us. He feels our pain and offers His comfort and support.

One of the most comforting aspects of Jesus knowing our sorrows is that He offers us His presence and companionship. When we are going through difficult times, it can feel like we are all alone in our pain. But Jesus is always with us, even in our darkest moments. He walks with us through our suffering, offering His love and comfort. Knowing that Jesus is with us can bring a great sense of peace and reassurance. We are never alone in our sorrows because Jesus is always by our side. His presence can provide strength and hope, helping us to endure and overcome our struggles.

Jesus's understanding of our sorrows also means that He offers us His healing. He knows the deep wounds that sorrow can leave in our hearts and souls. Whether it is emotional pain, mental anguish, or spiritual distress, Jesus offers His healing touch. He has the power to mend broken hearts, restore hope, and bring peace to troubled minds. His healing is not just about removing the pain but also about helping us to grow and find new strength in the midst of our suffering. Jesus's healing can transform our sorrows into opportunities for growth and deeper faith. By turning to Him, we can find the strength to move forward and find joy again.

Moreover, Jesus's knowledge of our sorrows includes His promise of comfort. In the Bible, Jesus says, "Blessed are they that mourn: for they shall be comforted" (Matthew 5:4). This promise assures us that our sorrow will not last forever and that Jesus will provide the comfort we need. He understands the depth of our pain and is committed to helping us through it. This comfort can come in many forms, such as a sense of peace, the support of loved ones, or a renewed sense of hope. Jesus's promise of comfort is a reminder that our sorrows are temporary and that His love and care are everlasting.

Understanding that Jesus knows our sorrows can also help us to be more compassionate towards others. Just as Jesus empathizes with our pain, we are called to empathize with the pain of those around us. By recognizing that everyone experiences sorrow, we can be more understanding and supportive. This empathy can help us to build stronger, more loving communities where people feel cared for and supported. Jesus's example of compassion teaches us to reach out to others in their times of need, offering our love and support just as He does for us.

Jesus's knowledge of our sorrows also includes His understanding of the different ways we cope with pain. Everyone deals with sorrow differently, and Jesus sees and understands our individual coping mechanisms. Whether we seek comfort in prayer, turn to friends and family, or find solace in nature or hobbies, Jesus knows what we need to heal and cope. His understanding helps us to find healthy and constructive ways to deal with our pain. He guides us towards activities and practices that can bring us peace and healing. By following His guidance, we can navigate our sorrows in a way that leads to growth and renewal.

Another important aspect of Jesus knowing our sorrows is His role as our advocate. Jesus not only understands our pain but also advocates for us before God the Father. He intercedes on our behalf, bringing our sorrows and needs to God. This advocacy is rooted in His deep love and compassion for us. Knowing that Jesus is advocating for us can bring us great comfort and reassurance. It means that our sorrows are seen and acknowledged by God, and that we are never forgotten or overlooked. Jesus's advocacy ensures that we are always in God's care, even in our times of deepest sorrow.

Furthermore, Jesus's knowledge of our sorrows highlights the importance of hope. In the midst of our pain, it can be difficult to see a way forward. But Jesus offers us the hope of a better future. His resurrection is a powerful reminder that sorrow and death do not have the final word. Through His victory over death, Jesus assures us that there is always hope, even in the darkest times. This hope can give us the strength to keep going, to persevere through our sorrows, and to trust that better days are ahead. Jesus's knowledge of our sorrows is a source of hope and encouragement, reminding us that we are never alone and that His love will see us through.

In addition to offering us hope, Jesus's knowledge of our sorrows teaches us the value of perseverance. Sorrow can be incredibly challenging, but it can also be an opportunity for growth and resilience. Jesus understands the strength it takes to persevere through difficult times, and He offers us His support and encouragement. By relying on His strength, we can find the courage to keep going, even when the road is tough. Jesus's example of enduring suffering with grace and faith inspires us to do the same. His presence in our lives gives us the fortitude to face our sorrows head-on and to emerge stronger on the other side.

Understanding that Jesus knows our sorrows can also deepen our faith. When we recognize that Jesus is intimately aware of our pain and is with us through it all, it can strengthen our trust in Him. This deepened faith can bring us closer to Jesus, helping us to rely on His guidance and support. Our relationship with Him can become a source of strength and comfort, providing a solid foundation to stand on in times of trouble. Jesus's knowledge of our sorrows is a testament to His unwavering love and commitment to us, fostering a deeper and more meaningful connection with Him.

In conclusion, understanding that the Lord knows all about our sorrows, as described in Isaiah 53:3, is a profound and comforting truth. Jesus's complete knowledge of our sorrows means that He is aware of every instance of pain and sadness in our lives. His own experiences with sorrow and rejection give Him a unique perspective on our suffering. Jesus's awareness of our sorrows includes His presence and companionship, His offer of healing, His promise of comfort, His example of compassion, His guidance for healthy coping, His advocacy before God, His assurance of hope, and His encouragement for perseverance. This comprehensive understanding of our sorrows can bring us great comfort and peace, knowing that we are fully known and fully loved by Jesus. It can inspire us to seek His comfort and healing, to be compassionate towards others, to find healthy ways to cope, to rely on His advocacy, to hold onto hope, to persevere through challenges, and to deepen our faith. Embracing this truth can transform our lives, fostering a deeper relationship with Jesus and a greater sense of peace, hope, and joy in our daily walk with Him. Jesus's knowledge of our sorrows is a testament to His divine wisdom, love, and compassion, offering us the opportunity for healing, growth, and transformation.

This understanding can change our lives, helping us to live in the light of His truth and love, and to become the people He created us to be.

Chapter 6 - Your Steps

"I know thy works, and thy labour, and thy patience..." (Revelation 2:2)

This verse tells us that Jesus, the Son of God, knows every step we take, every effort we make, and every act of patience we show. Jesus's knowledge of our steps means that He sees all our actions, understands our hard work, and recognizes our perseverance. This deep understanding is part of His divine nature. Knowing our steps means that Jesus is aware of everything we do in our daily lives, from the smallest tasks to the biggest challenges. Even when we think no one notices our efforts, Jesus sees and appreciates everything. This knowledge can be both comforting and motivating. On one hand, it means that we are fully known and understood by Jesus. He sees our true selves, including our struggles and successes. On the other hand, it reminds us that our actions matter and that Jesus values our hard work and dedication.

Jesus knowing our steps means He is aware of every decision we make and every path we choose. Life is full of choices, and sometimes it can be difficult to know which way to go. Jesus's knowledge of our steps assures us that He is always guiding us and helping us make the right decisions. He knows our goals, dreams, and desires, and He helps us to pursue them in ways that align with His will. This guidance is rooted in His deep love and care for us. Jesus wants us to succeed and fulfill our potential, and He is always there to support us. When we seek His guidance, we can trust that He will lead us on the right path.

One of the most comforting aspects of Jesus knowing our steps is His recognition of our hard work and efforts. Sometimes, it can feel like our efforts go unnoticed or unappreciated. But Jesus sees everything we do and values our dedication and perseverance. Whether it's studying hard for a test, working diligently at a job, or helping others in need, Jesus knows and appreciates our efforts. His recognition can be a great source of encouragement and motivation. Knowing that Jesus sees and values our hard work can inspire us to keep going, even when the road is tough.

Jesus's understanding of our steps also means that He is aware of the challenges and obstacles we face. Life is not always easy, and we all encounter difficulties along the way. Jesus knows our struggles and is always there to offer His support and strength. He understands the effort it takes to overcome obstacles and the patience required to persevere through tough times. His presence in our lives can provide us with the strength and courage we need to keep moving forward. By relying on His strength, we can face challenges with confidence and resilience.

Moreover, Jesus's knowledge of our steps includes His awareness of our successes and achievements. He sees the moments when we reach our goals and accomplish great things. These successes are not just personal victories; they are also a testament to Jesus's guidance and support in our lives. Knowing that Jesus shares in our joy can make our achievements even more meaningful. His acknowledgment of our successes can inspire us to continue striving for excellence and to use our talents and abilities for His glory.

Jesus's understanding of our steps also means that He is aware of our need for rest and balance. While hard work and dedication are important, it is also essential to take time for rest and self-care. Jesus knows when we are tired and in need of a break. He encourages us to find a healthy balance between work and rest. His guidance can help us to avoid burnout and to maintain our physical, emotional, and spiritual well-being. By following Jesus's example, we can find the right balance in our lives and ensure that we are taking care of ourselves as we pursue our goals.

Another important aspect of Jesus knowing our steps is His understanding of our relationships and interactions with others. He sees how we treat people, how we build and maintain relationships, and how we support and care for those around us. Jesus's knowledge of our interactions can guide us to be more loving, compassionate, and supportive in our relationships. His example of love and kindness can inspire us to treat others with respect and care. By following His teachings, we can build strong and meaningful connections with the people in our lives.

Understanding that Jesus knows all our steps can also deepen our faith and trust in Him. When we recognize that Jesus is aware of every aspect of our lives and is always guiding and supporting us, it can strengthen our relationship with Him. This deepened faith can bring us closer to Jesus and help us to rely on His guidance and support. Our relationship with Him can become a source of strength and comfort, providing a solid foundation to stand on in times of trouble. Jesus's knowledge of our steps is a testament to His unwavering love and commitment to us, fostering a deeper and more meaningful connection with Him.

Furthermore, Jesus's knowledge of our steps includes His understanding of our spiritual journey. He sees our efforts to grow in faith, our struggles with doubt, and our moments of spiritual breakthrough. Jesus knows the steps we take to strengthen our relationship with Him, such as praying, reading the Bible, and participating in church activities. His awareness of our spiritual journey assures us that He is always with us, helping us to grow and deepen our faith. By turning to Jesus for guidance and support, we can navigate our spiritual journey with confidence and assurance.

In addition to understanding our spiritual journey, Jesus's knowledge of our steps highlights the importance of perseverance and resilience. Life is full of ups and downs, and it can be easy to get discouraged when things don't go as planned. Jesus's understanding of our efforts and struggles reminds us that perseverance is key. He encourages us to keep going, even when the road is tough. His presence in our lives can provide the strength and determination we need to persevere through challenges and setbacks. By relying on Jesus's support, we can find the resilience to keep moving forward and to overcome obstacles.

Jesus's knowledge of our steps also includes His awareness of our need for purpose and fulfillment. He knows that we all have a desire to live meaningful lives and to use our talents and abilities to make a difference in the world. Jesus provides us with opportunities to fulfill this need by guiding us towards our unique purpose and calling. He knows our strengths and weaknesses and helps us to use them in ways that bring joy and fulfillment. His guidance ensures that we can live lives that are not only satisfying to us but also glorify Him and help others.

Moreover, understanding that Jesus knows our steps can inspire us to live with integrity and accountability. Knowing that Jesus sees all our actions can motivate us to make choices that reflect our faith and values. It can encourage us to be honest, responsible, and ethical in everything we do. Jesus's knowledge of our steps is a reminder that we are accountable for our actions and that our choices matter. By living with integrity, we can honor Jesus and build a life that is pleasing to Him.

In conclusion, understanding that the Lord knows all about our steps, as described in Revelation 2:2, is a profound and comforting truth. Jesus's complete knowledge of our steps means that He sees and understands every action we take, every effort we make, and every act of patience we show. His knowledge includes His recognition of our hard work and dedication, His support in our challenges and obstacles, His acknowledgment of our successes and achievements, His guidance for rest and balance, His awareness of our relationships and interactions, His support in our spiritual journey, His encouragement for perseverance and resilience, and His understanding of our need for purpose and fulfillment. This comprehensive understanding of our steps can bring us great comfort and motivation, knowing that we are fully known and fully loved by Jesus. It can inspire us to seek His guidance, to live with integrity and accountability, to find balance and rest, to build meaningful relationships, and to deepen our faith. Embracing this truth can transform our lives, fostering a deeper relationship with Jesus and a greater sense of peace, hope, and joy in our daily walk with Him. Jesus's knowledge of our steps is a testament to His divine wisdom, love, and compassion, offering us the opportunity for growth, fulfillment, and transformation. This understanding can change our lives, helping us to live in the light of His truth and love, and to become the people He created us to be.

Chapter 7 - Your Steadfastness

"When Jesus saw their faith, he said unto the sick of the palsy, Son, thy sins be forgiven thee." (Mark 2:5)

This verse shows that Jesus, the Son of God, recognizes and appreciates our faith and steadfastness. Steadfastness means being firm and unwavering in our faith and actions, even in the face of challenges and difficulties. Jesus's knowledge of our steadfastness means that He sees our dedication and perseverance in our spiritual journey. He understands our efforts to remain faithful and committed to Him, no matter what obstacles we encounter. This deep understanding is part of His divine nature. Knowing our steadfastness means that Jesus is aware of our consistent efforts to follow His teachings, live according to His will, and maintain our faith. Even when we face doubts, fears, or hardships, Jesus sees our steadfastness and values our commitment. This knowledge can be both comforting and motivating. On one hand, it means that we are fully known and understood by Jesus. He sees our true selves, including our struggles and successes. On the other hand, it reminds us that our faith and actions matter and that Jesus values our dedication and perseverance.

Jesus knowing our steadfastness means He is aware of every time we choose to trust Him and follow His path. Life is full of challenges that can test our faith, such as personal struggles, difficult decisions, and external pressures. Jesus's knowledge of our steadfastness assures us that He is always aware of our efforts to stay true to our faith. He knows when we make difficult choices to follow His teachings, even when it's not easy. His recognition of our steadfastness can be a great source of encouragement and motivation. Knowing that Jesus sees and values our faithfulness can inspire us to keep going, even when the road is tough.

One of the most comforting aspects of Jesus knowing our steadfastness is His recognition of our efforts to grow spiritually. Spiritual growth is a journey that requires dedication, patience, and perseverance. Sometimes, it can feel like our efforts go unnoticed or unappreciated. But Jesus sees everything we do to strengthen our faith and deepen our relationship with Him. Whether it's praying regularly, studying the Bible, attending church, or helping others, Jesus knows and appreciates our efforts. His recognition can be a great source of encouragement and motivation. Knowing that Jesus sees and values our spiritual growth can inspire us to keep striving to become better followers of Him.

Jesus's understanding of our steadfastness also means that He is aware of the challenges and obstacles we face in our spiritual journey. Life is not always easy, and we all encounter difficulties that can test our faith. Jesus knows our struggles and is always there to offer His support and strength. He understands the effort it takes to remain steadfast in our faith, especially when we face adversity. His presence in our lives can provide us with the strength and courage we need to keep moving forward. By relying on His strength, we can face challenges with confidence and resilience.

Moreover, Jesus's knowledge of our steadfastness includes His awareness of our successes and achievements in our spiritual journey. He sees the moments when we overcome doubts, make progress in our faith, and accomplish spiritual goals. These successes are not just personal victories; they are also a testament to Jesus's guidance and support in our lives. Knowing that Jesus shares in our joy can make our achievements even more meaningful. His acknowledgment of our spiritual successes can inspire us to continue striving for excellence and to use our talents and abilities for His glory.

Jesus's understanding of our steadfastness also means that He is aware of our need for encouragement and support. While remaining steadfast in our faith is important, it is also essential to seek encouragement and support from others. Jesus knows when we need a boost in our spiritual journey and provides us with the encouragement we need. His guidance can help us to find supportive communities and relationships that nurture our faith. By following Jesus's example, we can also offer encouragement and support to others, helping them to remain steadfast in their faith.

Another important aspect of Jesus knowing our steadfastness is His understanding of our relationships and interactions with others. He sees how we build and maintain relationships that are rooted in faith and love. Jesus's knowledge of our interactions can guide us to be more loving, compassionate, and supportive in our relationships. His example of love and kindness can inspire us to treat others with respect and care. By following His teachings, we can build strong and meaningful connections with the people in our lives and help each other remain steadfast in our faith.

Understanding that Jesus knows all our steadfastness can also deepen our faith and trust in Him. When we recognize that Jesus is aware of every aspect of our spiritual journey and is always guiding and supporting us, it can strengthen our relationship with Him. This deepened faith can bring us closer to Jesus and help us to rely on His guidance and support. Our relationship with Him can become a source of strength and comfort, providing a solid foundation to stand on in times of trouble. Jesus's knowledge of our steadfastness is a testament to His unwavering love and commitment to us, fostering a deeper and more meaningful connection with Him.

Furthermore, Jesus's knowledge of our steadfastness includes His understanding of our spiritual struggles and doubts. He sees the moments when we question our faith or feel distant from Him. Jesus understands that doubt is a natural part of our spiritual journey and offers us His support and guidance. His presence in our lives can help us to navigate our doubts and find answers to our spiritual questions. By turning to Jesus in times of doubt, we can find the reassurance and clarity we need to strengthen our faith and remain steadfast in our commitment to Him.

In addition to understanding our spiritual struggles, Jesus's knowledge of our steadfastness highlights the importance of perseverance and resilience in our faith journey. Life is full of ups and downs, and it can be easy to get discouraged when things don't go as planned. Jesus's understanding of our efforts and struggles reminds us that perseverance is key. He encourages us to keep going, even when the road is tough. His presence in our lives can provide the strength and determination we need to persevere through challenges and setbacks. By relying on Jesus's support, we can find the resilience to keep moving forward and to overcome obstacles in our spiritual journey.

Jesus's knowledge of our steadfastness also includes His awareness of our need for purpose and fulfillment in our spiritual journey. He knows that we all have a desire to live meaningful lives and to use our faith to make a difference in the world. Jesus provides us with opportunities to fulfill this need by guiding us towards our unique purpose and calling. He knows our strengths and weaknesses and helps us to use them in ways that bring joy and fulfillment. His guidance ensures that we can live lives that are not only satisfying to us but also glorify Him and help others.

Moreover, understanding that Jesus knows our steadfastness can inspire us to live with integrity and accountability in our faith journey. Knowing that Jesus sees all our efforts can motivate us to make choices that reflect our faith and values. It can encourage us to be honest, responsible, and ethical in everything we do. Jesus's knowledge of our steadfastness is a reminder that we are accountable for our actions and that our choices matter. By living with integrity, we can honor Jesus and build a life that is pleasing to Him.

In conclusion, understanding that the Lord knows all about our steadfastness, as described in Mark 2:5, is a profound and comforting truth. Jesus's complete knowledge of our steadfastness means that He sees and understands every effort we make to remain faithful and committed to Him. His knowledge includes His recognition of our spiritual growth, His support in our challenges and obstacles, His acknowledgment of our spiritual successes, His guidance for encouragement and support, His awareness of our relationships and interactions, His support in our spiritual struggles and doubts, His encouragement for perseverance and resilience, and His understanding of our need for purpose and fulfillment in our spiritual journey. This comprehensive understanding of our steadfastness can bring us great comfort and motivation, knowing that we are fully known and fully loved by Jesus. It can inspire us to seek His guidance, to live with integrity and accountability in our faith journey, to find encouragement and support, to build meaningful relationships, and to deepen our faith. Embracing this truth can transform our lives, fostering a deeper relationship with Jesus and a greater sense of peace, hope, and joy in our daily walk with Him. Jesus's knowledge of our steadfastness is a testament to His divine wisdom, love, and compassion, offering us the opportunity for spiritual growth, fulfillment, and transformation. This understanding can change our lives, helping us to live in the light of His truth and love, and to become the faithful and steadfast followers He created us to be.

Chapter 8 - Your Struggles

"Therefore I say unto you, Take no thought for your life, what ye shall eat, or what ye shall drink..." (Matthew 6:25)

This verse tells us that Jesus, the Son of God, is aware of all our struggles and worries. He knows the difficulties we face in life, including our daily concerns about food, clothing, and other necessities. Jesus's knowledge of our struggles means that He sees all our challenges, understands our fears, and recognizes our efforts to overcome them. This deep understanding is part of His divine nature. Knowing our struggles means that Jesus is aware of everything we go through, from the smallest worries to the biggest obstacles. Even when we feel overwhelmed and alone in our struggles, Jesus sees and cares about what we are experiencing. This knowledge can be both comforting and motivating. On one hand, it means that we are fully known and understood by Jesus. He sees our true selves, including our fears and hopes. On the other hand, it reminds us that our struggles matter to Jesus and that He is always there to help us.

Jesus knowing our struggles means He is aware of every worry and concern that weighs on our hearts. Life is full of challenges that can make us anxious and fearful, such as financial difficulties, health problems, relationship issues, and academic pressures. Jesus's knowledge of our struggles assures us that He is always aware of what we are going through. He knows our worries about the future, our fears about making mistakes, and our concerns about our loved ones. His awareness of our struggles can be a great source of comfort and motivation. Knowing that Jesus sees and cares about our struggles can inspire us to keep going, even when the road is tough.

One of the most comforting aspects of Jesus knowing our struggles is His promise of provision and care. In Matthew 6:25, Jesus tells us not to worry about our basic needs because He knows what we need and will provide for us. This promise assures us that we do not have to carry our burdens alone. Jesus is always there to support us and to meet our needs. His provision is not just about physical necessities like food and clothing but also about emotional and spiritual needs. Jesus knows when we need comfort, encouragement, and strength, and He provides these in abundance. His promise of provision can bring us great peace and reassurance, knowing that we are never alone in our struggles.

Jesus's understanding of our struggles also means that He is aware of the effort and perseverance it takes to overcome challenges. Life is not always easy, and we all encounter difficulties that require hard work and determination to overcome. Jesus sees our efforts to remain strong and to keep moving forward, even when things are tough. He understands the sacrifices we make and the resilience we show in the face of adversity. His presence in our lives can provide us with the strength and courage we need to keep going. By relying on His strength, we can face challenges with confidence and resilience.

Moreover, Jesus's knowledge of our struggles includes His awareness of our need for rest and balance. While it is important to work hard and persevere, it is also essential to take time for rest and self-care. Jesus knows when we are tired and in need of a break. He encourages us to find a healthy balance between work and rest. His guidance can help us to avoid burnout and to maintain our physical, emotional, and spiritual well-being. By following Jesus's example, we can find the right balance in our lives and ensure that we are taking care of ourselves as we navigate our struggles.

Another important aspect of Jesus knowing our struggles is His understanding of our relationships and interactions with others. He sees how we support and care for those around us, and how we seek support and care in return. Jesus's knowledge of our interactions can guide us to build strong and meaningful relationships that provide mutual support and encouragement. His example of love and kindness can inspire us to treat others with respect and compassion. By following

His teachings, we can create a network of support that helps us to navigate our struggles together.

Understanding that Jesus knows all our struggles can also deepen our faith and trust in Him. When we recognize that Jesus is aware of every aspect of our lives and is always guiding and supporting us, it can strengthen our relationship with Him. This deepened faith can bring us closer to Jesus and help us to rely on His guidance and support. Our relationship with Him can become a source of strength and comfort, providing a solid foundation to stand on in times of trouble. Jesus's knowledge of our struggles is a testament to His unwavering love and commitment to us, fostering a deeper and more meaningful connection with Him.

Furthermore, Jesus's knowledge of our struggles includes His understanding of our spiritual journey. He sees our efforts to grow in faith, our struggles with doubt, and our moments of spiritual breakthrough. Jesus knows the steps we take to strengthen our relationship with Him, such as praying, reading the Bible, and participating in church activities. His awareness of our spiritual journey assures us that He is always with us, helping us to grow and deepen our faith. By turning to Jesus for guidance and support, we can navigate our spiritual journey with confidence and assurance.

In addition to understanding our spiritual journey, Jesus's knowledge of our struggles highlights the importance of perseverance and resilience. Life is full of ups and downs, and it can be easy to get discouraged when things don't go as planned. Jesus's understanding of our efforts and struggles reminds us that perseverance is key. He encourages us to keep going, even when the road is tough. His presence in our lives can provide the strength and determination we need to persevere through challenges and setbacks. By relying on Jesus's support, we can find the resilience to keep moving forward and to overcome obstacles.

Jesus's knowledge of our struggles also includes His awareness of our need for purpose and fulfillment. He knows that we all have a desire to live meaningful lives and to use our talents and abilities to make a difference in the world. Jesus provides us with opportunities to fulfill this need by guiding us towards our unique purpose and calling. He knows our strengths and weaknesses and helps us to use them in ways that bring joy and fulfillment. His guidance ensures that we can live lives that are not only satisfying to us but also glorify Him and help others.

Moreover, understanding that Jesus knows our struggles can inspire us to live with integrity and accountability. Knowing that Jesus sees all our efforts can motivate us to make choices that reflect our faith and values. It can encourage us to be honest, responsible, and ethical in everything we do. Jesus's knowledge of our struggles is a reminder that we are accountable for our actions and that our choices matter. By living with integrity, we can honor Jesus and build a life that is pleasing to Him.

In conclusion, understanding that the Lord knows all about our struggles, as described in Matthew 6:25, is a profound and comforting truth. Jesus's complete knowledge of our struggles means that He sees and understands every worry, fear, and challenge we face. His knowledge includes His promise of provision and care, His support in our efforts and perseverance, His guidance for rest and balance, His awareness of our relationships and interactions, His support in our spiritual journey, His encouragement for perseverance and resilience, and His understanding of our need for purpose and fulfillment. This comprehensive understanding of our struggles can bring us great comfort and motivation, knowing that we are fully known and fully loved by Jesus. It can inspire us to seek His guidance, to live with integrity and accountability, to find balance and rest, to build meaningful relationships, and to deepen our faith. Embracing this truth can transform our lives, fostering a deeper relationship with Jesus and a greater sense of peace, hope, and joy in our daily walk with Him. Jesus's knowledge of our struggles is a testament to His divine wisdom, love, and compassion, offering us the opportunity for growth, fulfillment, and transformation. This understanding can change our lives, helping us to live in the light of His truth and love, and to become the people He created us to be.

Chapter 9 - Your Story

"For I know the thoughts that I think toward you, saith the Lord, thoughts of peace, and not of evil, to give you an expected end."
(Jeremiah 29:11)

This verse tells us that Jesus, the Son of God, knows every detail of our story—past, present, and future. He understands our unique journey and has a plan for our lives that is filled with hope and peace. Jesus's knowledge of our story means that He is aware of everything we have been through, everything we are currently experiencing, and everything that lies ahead. This deep understanding is part of His divine nature. Knowing our story means that Jesus is fully aware of our struggles, our triumphs, our fears, and our dreams. Even when we feel lost or unsure about our future, Jesus knows exactly where we are and where we are going. This knowledge can be both comforting and motivating. On one hand, it means that we are fully known and understood by Jesus. He sees our true selves, including our deepest thoughts and emotions. On the other hand, it reminds us that our lives have a purpose and that Jesus is guiding us toward a hopeful and meaningful future.

Jesus knowing our story means He is aware of every moment that has shaped us. Life is full of experiences that contribute to our unique journey, such as our upbringing, our education, our relationships, and our personal challenges. Jesus's knowledge of our story assures us that He sees all these experiences and understands how they have impacted us. He knows the moments of joy and celebration, as well as the times of pain and hardship. His awareness of our story can be a great source of comfort and motivation. Knowing that Jesus sees and cares about our entire journey can inspire us to keep going, even when the road is tough.

One of the most comforting aspects of Jesus knowing our story is His presence in every chapter of our lives. In Jeremiah 29:11, Jesus promises that His thoughts toward us are of peace and not of evil, to give us an expected end. This means that Jesus is always thinking about us and is actively involved in our lives. His presence provides us with the assurance that we are never alone. Jesus walks with us through every season, offering His love, guidance, and support. His presence can bring us great peace and reassurance, knowing that we are never alone in our journey.

Jesus's understanding of our story also means that He is aware of the specific plans and purposes He has for our lives. He has a unique plan for each of us, designed to bring us hope and fulfillment. Jesus knows the gifts and talents He has given us and the ways we can use them to make a difference in the world. His plan for our lives is not always easy to see, especially when we face challenges and uncertainties. But Jesus's knowledge of our story assures us that He is guiding us toward a future filled with purpose and meaning. By trusting in His plan, we can find the strength and confidence to pursue our dreams and live out our calling.

Moreover, Jesus's knowledge of our story includes His awareness of our growth and development. Life is a journey of continuous learning and growth, and Jesus sees every step of our progress. He knows the lessons we have learned, the skills we have developed, and the ways we have matured. His recognition of our growth can be a great source of encouragement and motivation. Knowing that Jesus sees and values our efforts to grow and improve can inspire us to keep striving to become the best versions of ourselves.

Jesus's understanding of our story also means that He is aware of the people and relationships that are part of our journey. He sees the family members, friends, mentors, and acquaintances who have influenced our lives. Jesus knows how these relationships have shaped us and understands the impact they have had on our story. His awareness of our relationships can guide us to build strong and meaningful connections with others. By following Jesus's example of love and kindness, we can nurture relationships that provide mutual support and encouragement.

Another important aspect of Jesus knowing our story is His understanding of our struggles and challenges. Life is not always easy, and we all face difficulties that test our faith and resilience. Jesus knows our struggles and is always there to offer His support and strength. He understands the effort it takes to overcome obstacles and the perseverance required to keep moving forward. His presence in our lives can provide us with the strength and courage we need to navigate our challenges. By relying on His strength, we can face difficulties with confidence and resilience.

Understanding that Jesus knows all our story can also deepen our faith and trust in Him. When we recognize that Jesus is aware of every aspect of our journey and is always guiding and supporting us, it can strengthen our relationship with Him. This deepened faith can bring us closer to Jesus and help us to rely on His guidance and support. Our relationship with Him can become a source of strength and comfort, providing a solid foundation to stand on in times of trouble. Jesus's knowledge of our story is a testament to His unwavering love and commitment to us, fostering a deeper and more meaningful connection with Him.

Furthermore, Jesus's knowledge of our story includes His understanding of our need for purpose and fulfillment. He knows that we all have a desire to live meaningful lives and to use our gifts and talents to make a difference in the world. Jesus provides us with opportunities to fulfill this need by guiding us toward our unique purpose and calling. He knows our strengths and weaknesses and helps us to use them in ways that bring joy and fulfillment. His guidance ensures that we can live lives that are not only satisfying to us but also glorify Him and help others.

Moreover, understanding that Jesus knows our story can inspire us to live with integrity and accountability. Knowing that Jesus sees all our actions and decisions can motivate us to make choices that reflect our faith and values. It can encourage us to be honest, responsible, and ethical in everything we do. Jesus's knowledge of our story is a reminder that we are accountable for our actions and that our choices matter. By living with integrity, we can honor Jesus and build a life that is pleasing to Him.

In conclusion, understanding that the Lord knows all about our story, as described in Jeremiah 29:11, is a profound and comforting truth. Jesus's complete knowledge of our story means that He sees and understands every detail of our journey. His knowledge includes His presence in every chapter of our lives, His specific plans and purposes for us, His awareness of our growth and development, His understanding of our relationships, His support in our struggles and challenges, His encouragement for perseverance and resilience, and His understanding of our need for purpose and fulfillment. This comprehensive understanding of our story can bring us great comfort and motivation, knowing that we are fully known and fully loved by Jesus. It can inspire us to seek His guidance, to live with integrity and accountability, to find purpose and fulfillment, to build meaningful relationships, and to deepen our faith. Embracing this truth can transform our lives, fostering a deeper relationship with Jesus and a greater sense of peace, hope, and joy in our daily walk with Him. Jesus's knowledge of our story is a testament to His divine wisdom, love, and compassion, offering us the opportunity for growth, fulfillment, and transformation. This understanding can change our lives, helping us to live in the light of His truth and love, and to become the people He created us to be.

Chapter 10 - Your Social Connections

"And he ordained twelve, that they should be with him, and that he might send them forth to preach." (Mark 3:14)

Understanding that the Lord knows everything about us, including our social connections, is incredibly comforting and powerful. In the Bible, Mark 3:14 (King James Version) says, "And he ordained twelve, that they should be with him, and that he might send them forth to preach." This verse shows that Jesus, the Son of God, recognizes the importance of relationships and social connections. Jesus chose twelve disciples to be with Him and to share His teachings, demonstrating His understanding of the value of companionship, community, and shared purpose. Knowing our social connections means that Jesus is aware of all the relationships in our lives, including our family, friends, classmates, teachers, neighbors, and everyone we interact with regularly. He understands how these relationships shape us, support us, and sometimes challenge us. Jesus sees the influence these connections have on our thoughts, actions, and overall well-being. This knowledge can be both comforting and motivating. On one hand, it means that we are fully known and understood by Jesus. He sees the people who bring us joy and those who may cause us pain. On the other hand, it reminds us that our relationships matter to Jesus and that He is always there to help us build strong, healthy, and supportive connections.

Jesus knowing our social connections means He is aware of every interaction and relationship we have. Life is full of various social interactions, from casual encounters to deep, meaningful relationships. Jesus's knowledge of our social connections assures us that He is always aware of who we spend our time with and how these interactions affect us. He knows our family dynamics, the friendships we cherish, the mentors who guide us, and even the conflicts we face with others. His awareness of our social connections can be a great source of comfort and motivation. Knowing that Jesus sees and cares about our relationships can inspire us to cultivate positive, supportive, and loving connections.

One of the most comforting aspects of Jesus knowing our social connections is His guidance in building and maintaining relationships. In Mark 3:14, Jesus chose His disciples to be with Him and to share in His mission. This shows that Jesus values community and the support of others in fulfilling our purpose. His example teaches us the importance of surrounding ourselves with people who share our values and support our growth. Jesus guides us in forming relationships that are based on mutual respect, love, and shared purpose. His guidance can help us to choose friends who encourage us, family members who support us, and mentors who inspire us. By following Jesus's example, we can build a network of relationships that enrich our lives and help us to grow.

Jesus's understanding of our social connections also means that He is aware of the challenges and conflicts we face in our relationships. Relationships are not always easy, and we all encounter difficulties with others from time to time. Jesus knows our struggles with misunderstandings, disagreements, and hurt feelings. He understands the pain of broken relationships and the effort it takes to mend them. His presence in our lives can provide us with the strength and wisdom we need to navigate these challenges. By relying on Jesus's guidance, we can find the courage to address conflicts, seek forgiveness, and work towards reconciliation. His example of love and forgiveness can inspire us to approach our relationships with grace and compassion.

Moreover, Jesus's knowledge of our social connections includes His awareness of our need for support and companionship. He knows that we all need people in our lives who we can rely on, confide in, and share our joys and sorrows with. Jesus provides us with the support we need by guiding us towards relationships that are nurturing and supportive. He encourages us to seek out friends and family members who uplift us and to be that source of support for others. By following Jesus's example of love and kindness, we can create a community of support that helps us to navigate the ups and downs of life.

Another important aspect of Jesus knowing our social connections is His understanding of our role in the lives of others. Just as Jesus chose His disciples to be with Him and to share His mission, He calls us to be a positive influence in the lives of those around us. He knows the impact we can have on our family, friends, classmates, and community. Jesus guides us to use our gifts and talents to serve others, to offer support and encouragement, and to share His love and teachings. By following His example, we can make a positive difference in the lives of others and help to build a loving and supportive community.

Understanding that Jesus knows all our social connections can also deepen our faith and trust in Him. When we recognize that Jesus is aware of every aspect of our relationships and is always guiding and supporting us, it can strengthen our relationship with Him. This deepened faith can bring us closer to Jesus and help us to rely on His guidance and support in our interactions with others. Our relationship with Him can become a source of strength and comfort, providing a solid foundation to stand on in times of social challenges and conflicts. Jesus's knowledge of our social connections is a testament to His unwavering love and commitment to us, fostering a deeper and more meaningful connection with Him.

Furthermore, Jesus's knowledge of our social connections includes His understanding of our need for purpose and fulfillment in our relationships. He knows that we all have a desire to connect with others in meaningful ways and to be part of a community that shares our values and goals. Jesus provides us with opportunities to fulfill this need by guiding us toward relationships that are purposeful and fulfilling. He knows our strengths and weaknesses and helps us to use them in ways that strengthen our relationships and bring joy and fulfillment. His guidance ensures that we can build relationships that are not only satisfying to us but also glorify Him and help others.

Moreover, understanding that Jesus knows our social connections can inspire us to live with integrity and accountability in our relationships. Knowing that Jesus sees all our interactions can motivate us to make choices that reflect our faith and values. It can encourage us to be honest, responsible, and ethical in everything we do. Jesus's knowledge of our social connections is a reminder that we are accountable for our actions and that our choices matter. By living with integrity, we can honor Jesus and build relationships that are pleasing to Him.

In conclusion, understanding that the Lord knows all about our social connections, as described in Mark 3:14, is a profound and comforting truth. Jesus's complete knowledge of our social connections means that He sees and understands every relationship and interaction we have. His knowledge includes His guidance in building and maintaining relationships, His support in navigating challenges and conflicts, His awareness of our need for support and companionship, His understanding of our role in the lives of others, His encouragement for purpose and fulfillment in our relationships, and His call for integrity and accountability in our interactions. This comprehensive understanding of our social connections can bring us great comfort and motivation, knowing that we are fully known and fully loved by Jesus. It can inspire us to seek His guidance, to build meaningful and supportive relationships, to live with integrity and accountability, and to deepen our faith. Embracing this truth can transform our lives, fostering a deeper relationship with Jesus and a greater sense of peace, hope, and joy in our daily interactions. Jesus's knowledge of our social connections is a testament to His divine wisdom, love, and compassion, offering us the opportunity for growth, fulfillment, and transformation in our relationships. This understanding can change our lives, helping us to live in the light of His truth and love, and to become the people He created us to be, connected in love and purpose with those around us.

Chapter 11 - Your Secrecy

"Delight thyself also in the Lord; and he shall give thee the desires of thine heart." (Psalm 37:4)

This verse shows that Jesus, the Son of God, knows our deepest desires and secrets, even those that we keep hidden from others. Jesus's knowledge of our secrecy means that He sees everything within us, including our innermost thoughts, feelings, and desires. This deep understanding is part of His divine nature. Knowing our secrecy means that Jesus is fully aware of our private struggles, hidden fears, unspoken dreams, and secret prayers. Even when we feel like no one understands us or knows what we are going through, Jesus does. This knowledge can be both comforting and motivating. On one hand, it means that we are fully known and understood by Jesus. He sees our true selves, including the parts we may be afraid to show to others. On the other hand, it reminds us that we do not have to carry our burdens alone because Jesus is always with us, ready to help and support us.

Jesus knowing our secrecy means He is aware of every hidden aspect of our lives. Life is full of moments and thoughts that we keep to ourselves, such as private worries, personal ambitions, and deep-seated fears. Jesus's knowledge of our secrecy assures us that He is always aware of what is going on inside our hearts and minds. He knows our private battles, the silent struggles we face, and the secret hopes we hold onto. His awareness of our secrecy can be a great source of comfort and motivation. Knowing that Jesus sees and cares about our hidden struggles can inspire us to be open and honest with Him, trusting that He will understand and help us through.

One of the most comforting aspects of Jesus knowing our secrecy is His understanding and compassion. In Psalm 37:4, we are encouraged to delight ourselves in the Lord, and He will give us the desires of our hearts. This means that Jesus not only knows our secret desires but also cares about fulfilling them in ways that are good for us. His compassion assures us that He wants the best for us and is willing to help us achieve our deepest desires. Jesus understands the fears and doubts that may prevent us from sharing our true selves with others, and He offers a safe space where we can be completely honest and vulnerable. His understanding can bring us great peace and reassurance, knowing that we are loved and accepted just as we are.

Jesus's understanding of our secrecy also means that He is aware of our need for privacy and personal space. While it is important to share our lives with others and build meaningful relationships, it is also essential to have moments of solitude and reflection. Jesus respects our need for privacy and provides us with the space to think, pray, and grow. His guidance can help us to find a healthy balance between openness and privacy, ensuring that we are taking care of our mental and emotional well-being. By following Jesus's example, we can learn to value and protect our personal space while also being open to sharing our lives with those we trust.

Moreover, Jesus's knowledge of our secrecy includes His awareness of our hidden talents and potential. He sees the gifts and abilities that we may not even recognize in ourselves. Jesus knows our strengths and weaknesses and understands how we can use our talents to make a positive impact in the world. His awareness of our potential can guide us to explore and develop our hidden talents, helping us to achieve our goals and fulfill our purpose. By trusting in Jesus's guidance, we can discover new abilities and opportunities that align with our deepest desires and passions.

Another important aspect of Jesus knowing our secrecy is His understanding of our hidden fears and anxieties. Life can be filled with uncertainties and challenges that cause us to worry and fear. Jesus knows these fears, even when we try to hide them from others or ourselves. His presence in our lives can provide us with the strength and courage we need to face our fears head-on. By relying on Jesus's support, we can find the confidence to overcome our anxieties and move forward with faith and trust. His understanding and compassion can bring us comfort, knowing that we are not alone in our struggles.

Understanding that Jesus knows all our secrecy can also deepen our faith and trust in Him. When we recognize that Jesus is aware of every hidden aspect of our lives and is always guiding and supporting us, it can strengthen our relationship with Him. This deepened faith can bring us closer to Jesus and help us to rely on His guidance and support. Our relationship with Him can become a source of strength and comfort, providing a solid foundation to stand on in times of uncertainty and doubt. Jesus's knowledge of our secrecy is a testament to His unwavering love and commitment to us, fostering a deeper and more meaningful connection with Him.

Furthermore, Jesus's knowledge of our secrecy includes His understanding of our need for authenticity and self-expression. He knows that we all have a desire to be true to ourselves and to live authentically. Jesus provides us with the encouragement and support we need to express our true selves, even when it feels difficult or scary. His guidance can help us to find the courage to share our thoughts and feelings honestly, without fear of judgment or rejection. By trusting in Jesus's love and acceptance, we can learn to embrace our true selves and live in a way that is true to our values and beliefs.

Moreover, understanding that Jesus knows our secrecy can inspire us to live with integrity and accountability. Knowing that Jesus sees all our hidden thoughts and actions can motivate us to make choices that reflect our faith and values. It can encourage us to be honest, responsible, and ethical in everything we do. Jesus's knowledge of our secrecy is a reminder that we are accountable for our actions and that our choices matter. By living with integrity, we can honor Jesus and build a life that is pleasing to Him.

In conclusion, understanding that the Lord knows all about our secrecy, as described in Psalm 37:4, is a profound and comforting truth. Jesus's complete knowledge of our secrecy means that He sees and understands every hidden aspect of our lives. His knowledge includes His understanding and compassion, His respect for our privacy and personal space, His awareness of our hidden talents and potential, His understanding of our hidden fears and anxieties, His encouragement for authenticity and self-expression, and His call for integrity and accountability. This comprehensive understanding of our secrecy can bring us great comfort and motivation, knowing that we are fully known and fully loved by Jesus. It can inspire us to seek His guidance, to be open and honest with Him, to find balance and privacy, to develop our hidden talents, to face our fears, to live authentically, and to deepen our faith. Embracing this truth can transform our lives, fostering a deeper relationship with Jesus and a greater sense of peace, hope, and joy in our daily walk with Him. Jesus's knowledge of our secrecy is a testament to His divine wisdom, love, and compassion, offering us the opportunity for growth, fulfillment, and transformation. This understanding can change our lives, helping us to live in the light of His truth and love, and to become the people He created us to be.

Chapter 12 - Your Supplications

"And when thou prayest, thou shalt not be as the hypocrites are..."
(Matthew 6:5)

This verse shows that Jesus, the Son of God, knows our prayers and the intentions behind them. Jesus's knowledge of our supplications means that He sees every prayer we offer, whether it is spoken aloud or whispered in our hearts. This deep understanding is part of His divine nature. Knowing our supplications means that Jesus is fully aware of our requests, our needs, our hopes, and our deepest desires. Even when we feel like no one is listening or understanding our prayers, Jesus does. This knowledge can be both comforting and motivating. On one hand, it means that we are fully known and understood by Jesus. He hears our cries for help, our pleas for guidance, and our expressions of gratitude. On the other hand, it reminds us that our prayers matter to Jesus and that He is always there to listen and respond.

Jesus knowing our supplications means He is aware of every prayer we offer, whether it is for ourselves, for others, or for the world. Life is full of moments that drive us to our knees in prayer, such as personal struggles, loved ones in need, and global issues that weigh heavily on our hearts. Jesus's knowledge of our supplications assures us that He is always aware of our prayers and understands the emotions and intentions behind them. He knows when we pray out of desperation, hope, joy, or sorrow. His awareness of our supplications can be a great source of comfort and motivation. Knowing that Jesus sees and cares about our prayers can inspire us to keep praying, even when we do not see immediate answers.

One of the most comforting aspects of Jesus knowing our supplications is His promise to listen and respond. In Matthew 6:5, Jesus emphasizes the importance of sincere prayer, not for show, but from the heart. This means that Jesus values genuine, heartfelt prayers and promises to respond to them in His perfect timing and according to His will. His promise assures us that our prayers do not go unheard and that He is actively working in our lives and the lives of those we pray for. Jesus's promise to listen and respond can bring us great peace and reassurance, knowing that we are never alone in our struggles and that He is always working for our good.

Jesus's understanding of our supplications also means that He is aware of our needs even before we ask. He knows the desires of our hearts, the struggles we face, and the help we seek. This intimate knowledge allows Him to provide exactly what we need, even when we do not know how to express it in words. Jesus's awareness of our needs ensures that He can answer our prayers in ways that are best for us, even if it is not what we initially expected. His understanding can bring us comfort, knowing that we are in the care of a loving and all-knowing Savior who is always looking out for our best interests.

Moreover, Jesus's knowledge of our supplications includes His awareness of the times we struggle with prayer. Prayer is a powerful and important part of our spiritual lives, but it can sometimes be difficult. We may struggle with finding the right words, staying focused, or even believing that our prayers make a difference. Jesus understands these struggles and offers His support and encouragement. He knows the effort it takes to come before Him in prayer and values our persistence and sincerity. By relying on Jesus's support, we can find the strength and motivation to continue praying, even when it feels challenging.

Another important aspect of Jesus knowing our supplications is His understanding of our gratitude and praise. Prayer is not just about asking for help; it is also about giving thanks and praising God for His goodness and blessings. Jesus knows the gratitude in our hearts and the joy we feel when we recognize His work in our lives. He understands the importance of expressing thanks and encourages us to cultivate a heart of gratitude. By following Jesus's example, we can make thanksgiving and praise a regular part of our prayer life, deepening our relationship with Him and strengthening our faith.

Understanding that Jesus knows all our supplications can also deepen our faith and trust in Him. When we recognize that Jesus is aware of every prayer we offer and is always guiding and supporting us, it can strengthen our relationship with Him. This deepened faith can bring us closer to Jesus and help us to rely on His guidance and support in our daily lives. Our relationship with Him can become a source of strength and comfort, providing a solid foundation to stand on in times of trouble. Jesus's knowledge of our supplications is a testament to His unwavering love and commitment to us, fostering a deeper and more meaningful connection with Him.

Furthermore, Jesus's knowledge of our supplications includes His understanding of our need for community and collective prayer. He knows that we are not meant to face life's challenges alone and that there is power in coming together in prayer. Jesus encourages us to pray with and for others, building a community of faith that supports and uplifts one another. His understanding of our need for community can guide us to seek out and nurture relationships with fellow believers, creating a network of support and encouragement. By praying together, we can strengthen our bonds and draw closer to Jesus as a community.

Moreover, understanding that Jesus knows our supplications can inspire us to live with integrity and accountability in our prayer lives. Knowing that Jesus sees the sincerity of our prayers can motivate us to approach prayer with honesty and humility. It can encourage us to be open and transparent with God, sharing our true thoughts and feelings without fear of judgment. Jesus's knowledge of our supplications is a reminder that we are accountable for our actions and that our prayers matter. By praying with integrity, we can honor Jesus and build a relationship with Him that is based on trust and authenticity.

In conclusion, understanding that the Lord knows all about our supplications, as described in Matthew 6:5, is a profound and comforting truth. Jesus's complete knowledge of our supplications means that He sees and understands every prayer we offer. His knowledge includes His promise to listen and respond, His awareness of our needs even before we ask, His support in our struggles with prayer, His understanding of our gratitude and praise, His encouragement for community and collective prayer, and His call for integrity and accountability in our prayer lives. This comprehensive understanding of our supplications can bring us great comfort and motivation, knowing that we are fully known and fully loved by Jesus. It can inspire us to seek His guidance, to pray with sincerity and honesty, to find strength and support in community, to live with integrity, and to deepen our faith. Embracing this truth can transform our lives, fostering a deeper relationship with Jesus and a greater sense of peace, hope, and joy in our daily walk with Him. Jesus's knowledge of our supplications is a testament to His divine wisdom, love, and compassion, offering us the opportunity for growth, fulfillment, and transformation in our prayer lives. This understanding can change our lives, helping us to live in the light of His truth and love, and to become the people He created us to be, connected in prayer and purpose with Him and with one another.

Chapter 13 - Your Sufferings

"These things I have spoken unto you, that in me ye might have peace. In the world ye shall have tribulation..." (John 16:33)

This verse shows that Jesus, the Son of God, is fully aware of the tribulations and sufferings we face in life. Jesus's knowledge of our sufferings means that He sees every pain, every hardship, and every tear we shed. This deep understanding is part of His divine nature. Knowing our sufferings means that Jesus is intimately aware of the physical, emotional, and spiritual pain we endure. Even when we feel like no one understands the depth of our pain, Jesus does. This knowledge can be both comforting and motivating. On one hand, it means that we are fully known and understood by Jesus. He sees our true selves, including our struggles and the burdens we carry. On the other hand, it reminds us that our suffering matters to Jesus and that He is always there to provide comfort, strength, and hope.

Jesus knowing our sufferings means He is aware of every trial and tribulation we face. Life is filled with challenges that can cause us to suffer, such as illness, loss, betrayal, and disappointment. Jesus's knowledge of our sufferings assures us that He is always aware of what we are going through. He knows the pain of losing a loved one, the frustration of dealing with a chronic illness, the heartbreak of a broken relationship, and the stress of financial difficulties. His awareness of our sufferings can be a great source of comfort and motivation. Knowing that Jesus sees and cares about our pain can inspire us to turn to Him for support and to trust that He is with us every step of the way.

One of the most comforting aspects of Jesus knowing our sufferings is His promise of peace and victory. In John 16:33, Jesus tells us that we will face tribulation in the world but assures us that we can have peace in Him because He has overcome the world. This promise means that Jesus offers us a peace that transcends our circumstances. His peace is not dependent on the absence of suffering but on His presence with us in the midst of it. Jesus's victory over the world and its tribulations assures us that our suffering is not the end of the story. His promise of peace and victory can bring us great reassurance and hope, knowing that we are not alone in our struggles and that He is working for our good.

Jesus's understanding of our sufferings also means that He is aware of the strength and resilience it takes to endure pain and hardship. Life's challenges can test our faith and perseverance, but Jesus sees our efforts to remain strong and to keep moving forward. He understands the courage it takes to face each day with hope and determination, even when the weight of suffering feels overwhelming. His presence in our lives can provide us with the strength and encouragement we need to persevere. By relying on Jesus's strength, we can find the resilience to endure our sufferings and to emerge stronger on the other side.

Moreover, Jesus's knowledge of our sufferings includes His awareness of our need for comfort and healing. He knows that suffering can leave deep wounds in our hearts and souls. Jesus offers us His healing touch, bringing comfort and restoration to our brokenness. His compassion assures us that He is with us in our pain, offering His love and support. Jesus's healing is not just about removing the pain but also about helping us to grow and find new strength in the midst of our suffering. His understanding and compassion can bring us comfort, knowing that we are not alone in our pain and that He is always working to bring healing and wholeness to our lives.

Another important aspect of Jesus knowing our sufferings is His understanding of the different ways we cope with pain. Everyone deals with suffering differently, and Jesus sees and understands our individual coping mechanisms. Whether we seek comfort in prayer, turn to friends and family, or find solace in nature or hobbies, Jesus knows what we need to heal and cope. His understanding helps us to find healthy and constructive ways to deal with our pain. He guides us towards activities and practices that can bring us peace and healing. By following His guidance, we can navigate our sufferings in a way that leads to growth and renewal.

Understanding that Jesus knows all our sufferings can also deepen our faith and trust in Him. When we recognize that Jesus is aware of every aspect of our pain and is always guiding and supporting us, it can strengthen our relationship with Him. This deepened faith can bring us closer to Jesus and help us to rely on His guidance and support. Our relationship with Him can become a source of strength and comfort, providing a solid foundation to stand on in times of trouble. Jesus's knowledge of our sufferings is a testament to His unwavering love and commitment to us, fostering a deeper and more meaningful connection with Him.

Furthermore, Jesus's knowledge of our sufferings includes His understanding of our need for purpose and meaning in the midst of pain. He knows that we all have a desire to understand why we suffer and to find meaning in our experiences. Jesus provides us with opportunities to find purpose in our suffering by guiding us towards ways to use our pain for good. He knows our strengths and weaknesses and helps us to use them in ways that bring healing and hope to others. His guidance ensures that our suffering is not in vain but can be transformed into a source of strength and inspiration for ourselves and others.

Moreover, understanding that Jesus knows our sufferings can inspire us to live with compassion and empathy towards others. Knowing that Jesus sees and understands our pain can motivate us to reach out to those who are suffering and offer our support and love. Jesus's example of compassion teaches us to be there for others in their times of need, to listen to their pain, and to offer a comforting presence. By following His example, we can create a community of support and encouragement, helping each other to navigate the challenges of life.

In conclusion, understanding that the Lord knows all about our sufferings, as described in John 16:33, is a profound and comforting truth. Jesus's complete knowledge of our sufferings means that He sees and understands every pain, hardship, and tear we shed. His knowledge includes His promise of peace and victory, His support in our strength and resilience, His awareness of our need for comfort and healing, His guidance in coping with pain, His understanding of our need for purpose and meaning, and His call for compassion and empathy towards others. This comprehensive understanding of our sufferings can bring us great comfort and motivation, knowing that we are fully known and fully loved by Jesus. It can inspire us to seek His guidance, to trust in His promise of peace and victory, to find strength and resilience in His presence, to seek comfort and healing in His love, to find purpose and meaning in our pain, to live with compassion and empathy, and to deepen our faith. Embracing this truth can transform our lives, fostering a deeper relationship with Jesus and a greater sense of peace, hope, and joy in our daily walk with Him. Jesus's knowledge of our sufferings is a testament to His divine wisdom, love, and compassion, offering us the opportunity for growth, fulfillment, and transformation in our experiences of pain and hardship. This understanding can change our lives, helping us to live in the light of His truth and love, and to become the people He created us to be, strengthened and healed by His presence in our sufferings.

Chapter 14 - Your Shortcomings

"For we have not an high priest which cannot be touched with the feeling of our infirmities..." (Hebrews 4:15)

This verse shows that Jesus, the Son of God, understands our weaknesses and shortcomings because He lived as a human and experienced the same temptations and struggles that we do. Jesus's knowledge of our shortcomings means that He sees every mistake, every failure, and every flaw in our lives. This deep understanding is part of His divine nature. Knowing our shortcomings means that Jesus is fully aware of our imperfections and the areas where we fall short. Even when we feel like no one understands our struggles or sees our efforts to improve, Jesus does. This knowledge can be both comforting and motivating. On one hand, it means that we are fully known and understood by Jesus. He sees our true selves, including our flaws and weaknesses. On the other hand, it reminds us that our shortcomings matter to Jesus and that He is always there to help us grow and improve.

Jesus knowing our shortcomings means He is aware of every time we stumble and fall. Life is full of challenges and temptations that can cause us to make mistakes and fail to live up to our own expectations and the expectations of others. Jesus's knowledge of our shortcomings assures us that He is always aware of our struggles and understands the difficulty of overcoming our weaknesses. He knows when we try our best and still fall short, and He sees the effort we put into trying to do better. His awareness of our shortcomings can be a great source of comfort and motivation. Knowing that Jesus sees and cares about our struggles can inspire us to turn to Him for support and to trust that He is with us every step of the way.

One of the most comforting aspects of Jesus knowing our shortcomings is His compassion and forgiveness. In Hebrews 4:15, we learn that Jesus is a high priest who can empathize with our weaknesses because He experienced the same temptations and struggles we face, yet without sin. This means that Jesus understands our weaknesses and offers us His compassion and forgiveness. His compassion assures us that He does not judge us harshly for our shortcomings but instead offers us His love and support. Jesus's forgiveness means that we can come to Him with our mistakes and failures, knowing that He will forgive us and help us to start anew. His compassion and forgiveness can bring us great peace and reassurance, knowing that we are loved and accepted just as we are.

Jesus's understanding of our shortcomings also means that He is aware of our efforts to overcome our weaknesses and grow. He sees the steps we take to improve ourselves, the changes we try to make, and the ways we seek to become better people. Jesus values our efforts and encourages us to keep striving for growth and improvement. His guidance can help us to find the strength and determination to overcome our shortcomings and to develop our strengths. By relying on Jesus's support, we can find the motivation to keep working on ourselves and to trust that He is helping us to become the people He created us to be.

Moreover, Jesus's knowledge of our shortcomings includes His awareness of our need for grace and mercy. He knows that we are not perfect and that we will make mistakes. Jesus offers us His grace and mercy, assuring us that we do not have to be perfect to be loved by Him. His grace means that we are accepted and loved despite our flaws and failures. Jesus's mercy means that He is always ready to forgive us and to give us another chance. His grace and mercy can bring us comfort, knowing that we are not alone in our struggles and that Jesus is always there to help us and to lift us up when we fall.

Another important aspect of Jesus knowing our shortcomings is His understanding of our potential for growth and transformation. He sees not only our current weaknesses but also the person we can become with His help. Jesus knows our strengths and abilities and understands how we can use them to overcome our shortcomings and to grow in our faith and character. His understanding helps us to see our potential and to believe in our ability to change and improve. By trusting in Jesus's guidance, we can discover new strengths and opportunities for growth that align with His plan for our lives.

Understanding that Jesus knows all our shortcomings can also deepen our faith and trust in Him. When we recognize that Jesus is aware of every aspect of our lives, including our flaws and weaknesses, and is always guiding and supporting us, it can strengthen our relationship with Him. This deepened faith can bring us closer to Jesus and help us to rely on His guidance and support. Our relationship with Him can become a source of strength and comfort, providing a solid foundation to stand on in times of trouble. Jesus's knowledge of our shortcomings is a testament to His unwavering love and commitment to us, fostering a deeper and more meaningful connection with Him.

Furthermore, Jesus's knowledge of our shortcomings includes His understanding of our need for encouragement and support. He knows that overcoming our weaknesses and growing in our faith can be challenging, and He offers us His encouragement and support every step of the way. Jesus encourages us to keep trying, even when we fail, and to trust in His ability to help us overcome our shortcomings. His support assures us that we are not alone in our struggles and that He is always there to help us and to lift us up. By relying on Jesus's encouragement and support, we can find the strength and motivation to keep moving forward and to trust that He is helping us to become the people He created us to be.

Moreover, understanding that Jesus knows our shortcomings can inspire us to live with integrity and accountability. Knowing that Jesus sees all our flaws and weaknesses can motivate us to be honest and humble about our struggles. It can encourage us to seek help and support from others and to take responsibility for our actions. Jesus's knowledge of our shortcomings is a reminder that we are accountable for our actions and that our choices matter. By living with integrity and accountability, we can honor Jesus and build a life that is pleasing to Him.

In conclusion, understanding that the Lord knows all about our shortcomings, as described in Hebrews 4:15, is a profound and comforting truth. Jesus's complete knowledge of our shortcomings means that He sees and understands every mistake, failure, and flaw in our lives. His knowledge includes His compassion and forgiveness, His support in our efforts to grow, His awareness of our need for grace and mercy, His understanding of our potential for growth and transformation, His encouragement and support, and His call for integrity and accountability. This comprehensive understanding of our shortcomings can bring us great comfort and motivation, knowing that we are fully known and fully loved by Jesus. It can inspire us to seek His guidance, to trust in His compassion and forgiveness, to find strength and determination in His support, to rely on His grace and mercy, to believe in our potential for growth, to live with integrity and accountability, and to deepen our faith. Embracing this truth can transform our lives, fostering a deeper relationship with Jesus and a greater sense of peace, hope, and joy in our daily walk with Him. Jesus's knowledge of our shortcomings is a testament to His divine wisdom, love, and compassion, offering us the opportunity for growth, fulfillment, and transformation in our journey of faith. This understanding can change our lives, helping us to live in the light of His truth and love, and to become the people He created us to be, strengthened and uplifted by His presence in our shortcomings.

Chapter 15 - Your Sacrifices

"And he looked up, and saw the rich men casting their gifts into the treasury." (Luke 21:1)

This verse shows that Jesus, the Son of God, is fully aware of the sacrifices we make, whether they are large or small. Jesus's knowledge of our sacrifices means that He sees every effort, every act of giving, and every moment of self-denial. This deep understanding is part of His divine nature. Knowing our sacrifices means that Jesus is fully aware of the things we give up, the efforts we put in to help others, and the times we put others' needs before our own. Even when we feel like no one notices or appreciates our sacrifices, Jesus does. This knowledge can be both comforting and motivating. On one hand, it means that we are fully known and understood by Jesus. He sees our true selves, including our willingness to make sacrifices for the good of others. On the other hand, it reminds us that our sacrifices matter to Jesus and that He is always there to recognize and reward our efforts.

Jesus knowing our sacrifices means He is aware of every time we give of ourselves, whether it is our time, our resources, our energy, or our love. Life is full of opportunities to make sacrifices, such as helping a friend in need, donating to charity, volunteering our time, or even making small daily sacrifices for the well-being of our family. Jesus's knowledge of our sacrifices assures us that He is always aware of our actions and understands the effort and love behind them. He knows when we go out of our way to help others, even when it is inconvenient or difficult. His awareness of our sacrifices can be a great source of comfort and motivation. Knowing that Jesus sees and cares about our efforts can inspire us to continue making sacrifices, even when it is challenging.

One of the most comforting aspects of Jesus knowing our sacrifices is His recognition and appreciation of them. In Luke 21:1, Jesus notices the rich men casting their gifts into the treasury, showing that He pays attention to our acts of giving. This means that Jesus values our sacrifices and acknowledges the love and generosity behind them. His recognition assures us that our efforts do not go unnoticed and that He appreciates every act of kindness and generosity. Jesus's appreciation can bring us great peace and reassurance, knowing that we are making a positive impact and that our sacrifices are meaningful and valued.

Jesus's understanding of our sacrifices also means that He is aware of the personal cost and effort involved. He knows that making sacrifices often requires us to give up something important to us, whether it is our time, our comfort, our resources, or our desires. Jesus sees the moments when we choose to put others first and the times when we give from our own need. His awareness of the personal cost of our sacrifices assures us that He understands the depth of our commitment and the love that motivates our actions. By recognizing the effort and cost involved, Jesus offers us His support and encouragement to continue making sacrifices for the good of others.

Moreover, Jesus's knowledge of our sacrifices includes His understanding of the impact they have on others. He sees how our acts of giving and self-denial benefit those around us and contribute to the greater good. Jesus understands that our sacrifices can bring hope, comfort, and support to others, and He values the positive impact we make. His understanding helps us to see the bigger picture and to appreciate the importance of our actions. By trusting in Jesus's guidance, we can be confident that our sacrifices are making a difference and that they are part of His plan for bringing love and goodness into the world.

Another important aspect of Jesus knowing our sacrifices is His understanding of our need for balance and self-care. While making sacrifices is important, it is also essential to take care of ourselves and to ensure that we do not become overwhelmed or exhausted. Jesus knows that we need to find a healthy balance between giving to others and taking care of our own needs. His guidance can help us to set boundaries, to recognize when we need rest, and to find ways to recharge and renew our strength. By following Jesus's example, we can learn to make sacrifices in a sustainable way that allows us to continue giving without burning out.

Understanding that Jesus knows all our sacrifices can also deepen our faith and trust in Him. When we recognize that Jesus is aware of every act of giving and self-denial and is always guiding and supporting us, it can strengthen our relationship with Him. This deepened faith can bring us closer to Jesus and help us to rely on His guidance and support in our daily lives. Our relationship with Him can become a source of strength and comfort, providing a solid foundation to stand on in times of difficulty and sacrifice. Jesus's knowledge of our sacrifices is a testament to His unwavering love and commitment to us, fostering a deeper and more meaningful connection with Him.

Furthermore, Jesus's knowledge of our sacrifices includes His understanding of our motivations and intentions. He knows the love and generosity that drive our actions, even when we do not receive recognition or praise from others. Jesus understands that our sacrifices are often made out of a desire to help and to make a positive impact. His understanding assures us that He values the purity and sincerity of our intentions, regardless of the outward acknowledgment we receive. By trusting in Jesus's knowledge of our hearts, we can be confident that our sacrifices are seen and appreciated by Him.

Moreover, understanding that Jesus knows our sacrifices can inspire us to live with integrity and accountability. Knowing that Jesus sees all our actions and understands our motivations can motivate us to make choices that reflect our faith and values. It can encourage us to be honest, responsible, and ethical in everything we do. Jesus's knowledge of our sacrifices is a reminder that we are accountable for our actions and that our choices matter. By living with integrity, we can honor Jesus and build a life that is pleasing to Him.

In conclusion, understanding that the Lord knows all about our sacrifices, as described in Luke 21:1, is a profound and comforting truth. Jesus's complete knowledge of our sacrifices means that He sees and understands every effort, every act of giving, and every moment of self-denial. His knowledge includes His recognition and appreciation, His awareness of the personal cost and effort involved, His understanding of the impact on others, His guidance for balance and self-care, His understanding of our motivations and intentions, and His call for integrity and accountability. This comprehensive understanding of our sacrifices can bring us great comfort and motivation, knowing that we are fully known and fully loved by Jesus. It can inspire us to seek His guidance, to trust in His recognition and appreciation, to find balance and self-care, to live with integrity and accountability, and to deepen our faith. Embracing this truth can transform our lives, fostering a deeper relationship with Jesus and a greater sense of peace, hope, and joy in our daily walk with Him. Jesus's knowledge of our sacrifices is a testament to His divine wisdom, love, and compassion, offering us the opportunity for growth, fulfillment, and transformation in our journey of faith. This understanding can change our lives, helping us to live in the light of His truth and love, and to become the people He created us to be, strengthened and uplifted by His presence in our sacrifices.

Chapter 16 - Your Service

"His lord said unto him, Well done, thou good and faithful servant..."
(Matthew 25:21)

This verse shows that Jesus, the Son of God, is fully aware of the service we render, whether it is small or significant. Jesus's knowledge of our service means that He sees every act of kindness, every effort to help others, and every moment of dedication. This deep understanding is part of His divine nature. Knowing our service means that Jesus is fully aware of the ways we contribute to the well-being of others and the sacrifices we make to serve. Even when we feel like no one notices or appreciates our service, Jesus does. This knowledge can be both comforting and motivating. On one hand, it means that we are fully known and understood by Jesus. He sees our true selves, including our willingness to serve others selflessly. On the other hand, it reminds us that our service matters to Jesus and that He is always there to recognize and reward our efforts.

Jesus knowing our service means He is aware of every time we lend a helping hand, whether it is in our community, our church, our school, or even our own homes. Life is full of opportunities to serve, such as volunteering at a local shelter, helping a neighbor with their groceries, tutoring a classmate, or taking care of a family member. Jesus's knowledge of our service assures us that He is always aware of our actions and understands the effort and love behind them. He knows when we go out of our way to help others, even when it is inconvenient or challenging. His awareness of our service can be a great source of comfort and motivation. Knowing that Jesus sees and cares about our efforts can inspire us to continue serving, even when it is difficult.

One of the most comforting aspects of Jesus knowing our service is His recognition and appreciation of it. In Matthew 25:21, Jesus commends the faithful servant, saying, "Well done, thou good and faithful servant." This means that Jesus values our service and acknowledges the love and dedication behind it. His recognition assures us that our efforts do not go unnoticed and that He appreciates every act of kindness and generosity. Jesus's appreciation can bring us great peace and reassurance, knowing that we are making a positive impact and that our service is meaningful and valued.

Jesus's understanding of our service also means that He is aware of the personal sacrifices and efforts involved. He knows that serving others often requires us to give up our time, our resources, our comfort, or our personal desires. Jesus sees the moments when we choose to put others first and the times when we serve from our own need. His awareness of the personal cost of our service assures us that He understands the depth of our commitment and the love that motivates our actions. By recognizing the effort and cost involved, Jesus offers us His support and encouragement to continue serving for the good of others.

Moreover, Jesus's knowledge of our service includes His understanding of the impact it has on others. He sees how our acts of service benefit those around us and contribute to the greater good. Jesus understands that our service can bring hope, comfort, and support to others, and He values the positive impact we make. His understanding helps us to see the bigger picture and to appreciate the importance of our actions. By trusting in Jesus's guidance, we can be confident that our service is making a difference and that it is part of His plan for bringing love and goodness into the world.

Another important aspect of Jesus knowing our service is His understanding of our need for balance and self-care. While serving others is important, it is also essential to take care of ourselves and ensure that we do not become overwhelmed or exhausted. Jesus knows that we need to find a healthy balance between serving others and taking care of our own needs. His guidance can help us to set boundaries, to recognize when we need rest, and to find ways to recharge and renew our strength. By following Jesus's example, we can learn to serve in a sustainable way that allows us to continue giving without burning out.

Understanding that Jesus knows all our service can also deepen our faith and trust in Him. When we recognize that Jesus is aware of every act of service and is always guiding and supporting us, it can strengthen our relationship with Him. This deepened faith can bring us closer to Jesus and help us to rely on His guidance and support in our daily lives. Our relationship with Him can become a source of strength and comfort, providing a solid foundation to stand on in times of difficulty and service. Jesus's knowledge of our service is a testament to His unwavering love and commitment to us, fostering a deeper and more meaningful connection with Him.

Furthermore, Jesus's knowledge of our service includes His understanding of our motivations and intentions. He knows the love and generosity that drive our actions, even when we do not receive recognition or praise from others. Jesus understands that our service is often motivated by a desire to help and to make a positive impact. His understanding assures us that He values the purity and sincerity of our intentions, regardless of the outward acknowledgment we receive. By trusting in Jesus's knowledge of our hearts, we can be confident that our service is seen and appreciated by Him.

Moreover, understanding that Jesus knows our service can inspire us to live with integrity and accountability. Knowing that Jesus sees all our actions and understands our motivations can motivate us to make choices that reflect our faith and values. It can encourage us to be honest, responsible, and ethical in everything we do. Jesus's knowledge of our service is a reminder that we are accountable for our actions and that our choices matter. By living with integrity, we can honor Jesus and build a life that is pleasing to Him.

In conclusion, understanding that the Lord knows all about our service, as described in Matthew 25:21, is a profound and comforting truth. Jesus's complete knowledge of our service means that He sees and understands every act of kindness, every effort to help others, and every moment of dedication. His knowledge includes His recognition and appreciation, His awareness of the personal sacrifices and efforts involved, His understanding of the impact on others, His guidance for balance and self-care, His understanding of our motivations and intentions, and His call for integrity and accountability. This comprehensive understanding of our service can bring us great comfort and motivation, knowing that we are fully known and fully loved by Jesus. It can inspire us to seek His guidance, to trust in His recognition and appreciation, to find balance and self-care, to live with integrity and accountability, and to deepen our faith. Embracing this truth can transform our lives, fostering a deeper relationship with Jesus and a greater sense of peace, hope, and joy in our daily walk with Him. Jesus's knowledge of our service is a testament to His divine wisdom, love, and compassion, offering us the opportunity for growth, fulfillment, and transformation in our journey of faith. This understanding can change our lives, helping us to live in the light of His truth and love, and to become the people He created us to be, strengthened and uplifted by His presence in our service.

Chapter 17 - Your Sacrifice

"For God is not unrighteous to forget your work and labour of love..."
(Hebrews 6:10)

Understanding that the Lord knows everything about us, including our sacrifices, is incredibly comforting and powerful. In the Bible, Hebrews 6:10 (King James Version) says, "For God is not unrighteous to forget your work and labour of love, which ye have shewed toward his name, in that ye have ministered to the saints, and do minister." This verse shows that Jesus, the Son of God, is fully aware of the sacrifices we make, whether they are large or small. Jesus's knowledge of our sacrifices means that He sees every effort, every act of giving, and every moment of self-denial. This deep understanding is part of His divine nature. Knowing our sacrifices means that Jesus is fully aware of the things we give up, the efforts we put in to help others, and the times we put others' needs before our own. Even when we feel like no one notices or appreciates our sacrifices, Jesus does. This knowledge can be both comforting and motivating. On one hand, it means that we are fully known and understood by Jesus. He sees our true selves, including our willingness to make sacrifices for the good of others. On the other hand, it reminds us that our sacrifices matter to Jesus and that He is always there to recognize and reward our efforts.

Jesus knowing our sacrifices means He is aware of every time we give of ourselves, whether it is our time, our resources, our energy, or our love. Life is full of opportunities to make sacrifices, such as helping a friend in need, donating to charity, volunteering our time, or even making small daily sacrifices for the well-being of our family. Jesus's knowledge of our sacrifices assures us that He is always aware of our actions and understands the effort and love behind them. He knows when we go out of our way to help others, even when it is inconvenient or difficult. His awareness of our sacrifices can be a great source of comfort and motivation. Knowing that Jesus sees and cares about our efforts can inspire us to continue making sacrifices, even when it is challenging.

One of the most comforting aspects of Jesus knowing our sacrifices is His recognition and appreciation of them. In Hebrews 6:10, it is clear that God does not forget our work and labor of love. This means that Jesus values our sacrifices and acknowledges the love and generosity behind them. His recognition assures us that our efforts do not go unnoticed and that He appreciates every act of kindness and generosity. Jesus's appreciation can bring us great peace and reassurance, knowing that we are making a positive impact and that our sacrifices are meaningful and valued.

Jesus's understanding of our sacrifices also means that He is aware of the personal cost and effort involved. He knows that making sacrifices often requires us to give up something important to us, whether it is our time, our comfort, our resources, or our desires. Jesus sees the moments when we choose to put others first and the times when we give from our own need. His awareness of the personal cost of our sacrifices assures us that He understands the depth of our commitment and the love that motivates our actions. By recognizing the effort and cost involved, Jesus offers us His support and encouragement to continue making sacrifices for the good of others.

Moreover, Jesus's knowledge of our sacrifices includes His understanding of the impact they have on others. He sees how our acts of giving and self-denial benefit those around us and contribute to the greater good. Jesus understands that our sacrifices can bring hope, comfort, and support to others, and He values the positive impact we make. His understanding helps us to see the bigger picture and to appreciate the importance of our actions. By trusting in Jesus's guidance, we can be confident that our sacrifices are making a difference and that they are part of His plan for bringing love and goodness into the world.

Another important aspect of Jesus knowing our sacrifices is His understanding of our need for balance and self-care. While making sacrifices is important, it is also essential to take care of ourselves and to ensure that we do not become overwhelmed or exhausted. Jesus knows that we need to find a healthy balance between giving to others and taking care of our own needs. His guidance can help us to set boundaries, to recognize when we need rest, and to find ways to recharge and renew our strength. By following Jesus's example, we can learn to make sacrifices in a sustainable way that allows us to continue giving without burning out.

Understanding that Jesus knows all our sacrifices can also deepen our faith and trust in Him. When we recognize that Jesus is aware of every act of giving and self-denial and is always guiding and supporting us, it can strengthen our relationship with Him. This deepened faith can bring us closer to Jesus and help us to rely on His guidance and support in our daily lives. Our relationship with Him can become a source of strength and comfort, providing a solid foundation to stand on in times of difficulty and sacrifice. Jesus's knowledge of our sacrifices is a testament to His unwavering love and commitment to us, fostering a deeper and more meaningful connection with Him.

Furthermore, Jesus's knowledge of our sacrifices includes His understanding of our motivations and intentions. He knows the love and generosity that drive our actions, even when we do not receive recognition or praise from others. Jesus understands that our sacrifices are often made out of a desire to help and to make a positive impact. His understanding assures us that He values the purity and sincerity of our intentions, regardless of the outward acknowledgment we receive. By trusting in Jesus's knowledge of our hearts, we can be confident that our sacrifices are seen and appreciated by Him.

Moreover, understanding that Jesus knows our sacrifices can inspire us to live with integrity and accountability. Knowing that Jesus sees all our actions and understands our motivations can motivate us to make choices that reflect our faith and values. It can encourage us to be honest, responsible, and ethical in everything we do. Jesus's knowledge of our sacrifices is a reminder that we are accountable for our actions and that our choices matter. By living with integrity, we can honor Jesus and build a life that is pleasing to Him.

In conclusion, understanding that the Lord knows all about our sacrifices, as described in Hebrews 6:10, is a profound and comforting truth. Jesus's complete knowledge of our sacrifices means that He sees and understands every effort, every act of giving, and every moment of self-denial. His knowledge includes His recognition and appreciation, His awareness of the personal cost and effort involved, His understanding of the impact on others, His guidance for balance and self-care, His understanding of our motivations and intentions, and His call for integrity and accountability. This comprehensive understanding of our sacrifices can bring us great comfort and motivation, knowing that we are fully known and fully loved by Jesus. It can inspire us to seek His guidance, to trust in His recognition and appreciation, to find balance and self-care, to live with integrity and accountability, and to deepen our faith. Embracing this truth can transform our lives, fostering a deeper relationship with Jesus and a greater sense of peace, hope, and joy in our daily walk with Him. Jesus's knowledge of our sacrifices is a testament to His divine wisdom, love, and compassion, offering us the opportunity for growth, fulfillment, and transformation in our journey of faith. This understanding can change our lives, helping us to live in the light of His truth and love, and to become the people He created us to be, strengthened and uplifted by His presence in our sacrifices.

Chapter 18 - Your Submission

"If ye love me, keep my commandments." (John 14:15)
This verse shows that Jesus, the Son of God, understands and values our acts of submission and obedience to His will. Jesus's knowledge of our submission means that He sees every time we choose to follow His commandments, even when it is difficult or goes against our personal desires. This deep understanding is part of His divine nature. Knowing our submission means that Jesus is fully aware of our efforts to live according to His teachings, to prioritize His will over our own, and to show our love for Him through our actions. Even when we feel like our struggles to obey go unnoticed, Jesus does notice. This knowledge can be both comforting and motivating. On one hand, it means that we are fully known and understood by Jesus. He sees our true selves, including our willingness to submit to His guidance. On the other hand, it reminds us that our submission matters to Jesus and that He is always there to help us stay faithful.

Jesus knowing our submission means He is aware of every time we choose His path over our own, whether it is in our decisions, our actions, or our thoughts. Life is full of opportunities to submit to God's will, such as choosing to forgive someone who has wronged us, deciding to act with kindness instead of anger, or taking the time to pray and read the Bible regularly. Jesus's knowledge of our submission assures us that He is always aware of our efforts and understands the sacrifices we make to follow Him. He knows when we resist temptation, when we choose integrity over dishonesty, and when we put others' needs before our own. His awareness of our submission can be a great source of comfort and motivation. Knowing that Jesus sees and values our obedience can inspire us to continue striving to live according to His teachings, even when it is challenging.

One of the most comforting aspects of Jesus knowing our submission is His appreciation and recognition of it. In John 14:15,

Jesus emphasizes that our love for Him is shown through our obedience to His commandments. This means that Jesus values our acts of submission and acknowledges the love and dedication behind them. His recognition assures us that our efforts to obey do not go unnoticed and that He appreciates every act of faithfulness. Jesus's appreciation can bring us great peace and reassurance, knowing that our submission is meaningful and valued.

Jesus's understanding of our submission also means that He is aware of the personal challenges and struggles involved. He knows that following His commandments often requires us to go against our natural inclinations, to make difficult choices, and to endure hardships. Jesus sees the moments when we choose to follow His will, even when it is difficult or uncomfortable. His awareness of the personal cost of our submission assures us that He understands the depth of our commitment and the love that motivates our actions. By recognizing the effort and sacrifices involved, Jesus offers us His support and encouragement to continue submitting to His will.

Moreover, Jesus's knowledge of our submission includes His understanding of the positive impact it has on our lives and the lives of others. He sees how our acts of obedience and submission to His will bring blessings, growth, and positive change. Jesus understands that our submission can lead to greater peace, joy, and fulfillment in our own lives, as well as in the lives of those we serve and influence. His understanding helps us to see the bigger picture and to appreciate the importance of our actions. By trusting in Jesus's guidance, we can be confident that our submission is making a difference and that it is part of His plan for bringing love and goodness into the world.

Another important aspect of Jesus knowing our submission is His understanding of our need for strength and perseverance. While submitting to God's will is important, it is also essential to have the strength and perseverance to continue following His commandments, even in the face of adversity. Jesus knows that we need His strength to remain faithful and to overcome the challenges we face. His guidance can help us to find the strength and determination to continue submitting to His will, even when it is difficult. By following Jesus's example, we can learn to rely on His strength and to trust in His guidance as we navigate the challenges of life.

Understanding that Jesus knows all our submission can also deepen our faith and trust in Him. When we recognize that Jesus is aware of every act of obedience and submission and is always guiding and supporting us, it can strengthen our relationship with Him. This deepened faith can bring us closer to Jesus and help us to rely on His guidance and support in our daily lives. Our relationship with Him can become a source of strength and comfort, providing a solid foundation to stand on in times of difficulty and temptation. Jesus's knowledge of our submission is a testament to His unwavering love and commitment to us, fostering a deeper and more meaningful connection with Him.

Furthermore, Jesus's knowledge of our submission includes His understanding of our motivations and intentions. He knows the love and dedication that drive our actions, even when we do not receive recognition or praise from others. Jesus understands that our submission is often motivated by a desire to honor Him and to live according to His will. His understanding assures us that He values the purity and sincerity of our intentions, regardless of the outward acknowledgment we receive. By trusting in Jesus's knowledge of our hearts, we can be confident that our submission is seen and appreciated by Him.

Moreover, understanding that Jesus knows our submission can inspire us to live with integrity and accountability. Knowing that Jesus sees all our actions and understands our motivations can motivate us to make choices that reflect our faith and values. It can encourage us to be honest, responsible, and ethical in everything we do. Jesus's knowledge of our submission is a reminder that we are accountable for our actions and that our choices matter. By living with integrity, we can honor Jesus and build a life that is pleasing to Him.

In conclusion, understanding that the Lord knows all about our submission, as described in John 14:15, is a profound and comforting truth. Jesus's complete knowledge of our submission means that He sees and understands every act of obedience and every moment of dedication to His will. His knowledge includes His recognition and appreciation, His awareness of the personal challenges and struggles involved, His understanding of the positive impact of our submission, His guidance for strength and perseverance, His understanding of our motivations and intentions, and His call for integrity and accountability. This comprehensive understanding of our submission can bring us great comfort and motivation, knowing that we are fully known and fully loved by Jesus. It can inspire us to seek His guidance, to trust in His recognition and appreciation, to find strength and perseverance, to live with integrity and accountability, and to deepen our faith. Embracing this truth can transform our lives, fostering a deeper relationship with Jesus and a greater sense of peace, hope, and joy in our daily walk with Him. Jesus's knowledge of our submission is a testament to His divine wisdom, love, and compassion, offering us the opportunity for growth, fulfillment, and transformation in our journey of faith. This understanding can change our lives, helping us to live in the light of His truth and love, and to become the people He created us to be, strengthened and uplifted by His presence in our submission.

Chapter 19 - Your Sufferings

"Blessed are they which are persecuted for righteousness' sake..."
(Matthew 5:10)

This verse shows that Jesus, the Son of God, is fully aware of the sufferings we endure, especially when we face persecution for doing what is right. Jesus's knowledge of our sufferings means that He sees every pain, every hardship, and every moment of persecution we endure for righteousness' sake. This deep understanding is part of His divine nature. Knowing our sufferings means that Jesus is intimately aware of the physical, emotional, and spiritual pain we experience. Even when we feel like no one understands the depth of our suffering, Jesus does. This knowledge can be both comforting and motivating. On one hand, it means that we are fully known and understood by Jesus. He sees our true selves, including our struggles and the burdens we carry. On the other hand, it reminds us that our suffering matters to Jesus and that He is always there to provide comfort, strength, and hope.

Jesus knowing our sufferings means He is aware of every trial and tribulation we face, especially when we suffer for doing what is right. Life is filled with challenges that can cause us to suffer, such as standing up for our beliefs, defending the truth, and acting with integrity in the face of opposition. Jesus's knowledge of our sufferings assures us that He is always aware of what we are going through. He knows the pain of being misunderstood, the frustration of facing injustice, the heartbreak of rejection, and the stress of standing alone. His awareness of our sufferings can be a great source of comfort and motivation. Knowing that Jesus sees and cares about our pain can inspire us to turn to Him for support and to trust that He is with us every step of the way.

One of the most comforting aspects of Jesus knowing our sufferings is His promise of blessing and reward. In Matthew 5:10, Jesus tells us that those who are persecuted for righteousness' sake are blessed and that the kingdom of heaven belongs to them. This promise means that Jesus offers us a future filled with hope and reward, even when we face suffering in the present. His promise assures us that our suffering is not in vain and that He recognizes and values our perseverance and faithfulness. Jesus's promise of blessing and reward can bring us great reassurance and hope, knowing that we are not alone in our struggles and that He is working for our good.

Jesus's understanding of our sufferings also means that He is aware of the strength and resilience it takes to endure pain and hardship. Life's challenges can test our faith and perseverance, but Jesus sees our efforts to remain strong and to keep moving forward. He understands the courage it takes to face each day with hope and determination, even when the weight of suffering feels overwhelming. His presence in our lives can provide us with the strength and encouragement we need to persevere. By relying on Jesus's strength, we can find the resilience to endure our sufferings and to emerge stronger on the other side.

Moreover, Jesus's knowledge of our sufferings includes His awareness of our need for comfort and healing. He knows that suffering can leave deep wounds in our hearts and souls. Jesus offers us His healing touch, bringing comfort and restoration to our brokenness. His compassion assures us that He is with us in our pain, offering His love and support. Jesus's healing is not just about removing the pain but also about helping us to grow and find new strength in the midst of our suffering. His understanding and compassion can bring us comfort, knowing that we are not alone in our pain and that He is always working to bring healing and wholeness to our lives.

Another important aspect of Jesus knowing our sufferings is His understanding of the different ways we cope with pain. Everyone deals with suffering differently, and Jesus sees and understands our individual coping mechanisms. Whether we seek comfort in prayer, turn to friends and family, or find solace in nature or hobbies, Jesus knows what we need to heal and cope. His understanding helps us to find healthy and constructive ways to deal with our pain. He guides us towards activities and practices that can bring us peace and healing. By following His guidance, we can navigate our sufferings in a way that leads to growth and renewal.

Understanding that Jesus knows all our sufferings can also deepen our faith and trust in Him. When we recognize that Jesus is aware of every aspect of our pain and is always guiding and supporting us, it can strengthen our relationship with Him. This deepened faith can bring us closer to Jesus and help us to rely on His guidance and support. Our relationship with Him can become a source of strength and comfort, providing a solid foundation to stand on in times of trouble. Jesus's knowledge of our sufferings is a testament to His unwavering love and commitment to us, fostering a deeper and more meaningful connection with Him.

Furthermore, Jesus's knowledge of our sufferings includes His understanding of our need for purpose and meaning in the midst of pain. He knows that we all have a desire to understand why we suffer and to find meaning in our experiences. Jesus provides us with opportunities to find purpose in our suffering by guiding us towards ways to use our pain for good. He knows our strengths and weaknesses and helps us to use them in ways that bring healing and hope to others. His guidance ensures that our suffering is not in vain but can be transformed into a source of strength and inspiration for ourselves and others.

Moreover, understanding that Jesus knows our sufferings can inspire us to live with compassion and empathy towards others. Knowing that Jesus sees and understands our pain can motivate us to reach out to those who are suffering and offer our support and love. Jesus's example of compassion teaches us to be there for others in their times of need, to listen to their pain, and to offer a comforting presence. By following His example, we can create a community of support and encouragement, helping each other to navigate the challenges of life.

In conclusion, understanding that the Lord knows all about our sufferings, as described in Matthew 5:10, is a profound and comforting truth. Jesus's complete knowledge of our sufferings means that He sees and understands every pain, hardship, and moment of persecution we endure for righteousness' sake. His knowledge includes His promise of blessing and reward, His support in our strength and resilience, His awareness of our need for comfort and healing, His guidance in coping with pain, His understanding of our need for purpose and meaning, and His call for compassion and empathy towards others. This comprehensive understanding of our sufferings can bring us great comfort and motivation, knowing that we are fully known and fully loved by Jesus. It can inspire us to seek His guidance, to trust in His promise of blessing and reward, to find strength and resilience in His presence, to seek comfort and healing in His love, to find purpose and meaning in our pain, to live with compassion and empathy, and to deepen our faith. Embracing this truth can transform our lives, fostering a deeper relationship with Jesus and a greater sense of peace, hope, and joy in our daily walk with Him. Jesus's knowledge of our sufferings is a testament to His divine wisdom, love, and compassion, offering us the opportunity for growth, fulfillment, and transformation in our experiences of pain and hardship. This understanding can change our lives, helping us to live in the light of His truth and love, and to become the people He created us to be, strengthened and healed by His presence in our sufferings.

Chapter 20 - Your Servanthood

"And whosoever will be chief among you, let him be your servant."
(Matthew 20:27)

This verse shows that Jesus, the Son of God, values servanthood and understands the importance of humility and service to others. Jesus's knowledge of our servanthood means that He sees every act of service, every moment of humility, and every effort we make to put others before ourselves. This deep understanding is part of His divine nature. Knowing our servanthood means that Jesus is fully aware of the ways we serve others, the sacrifices we make, and the times we choose to put others' needs before our own. Even when we feel like no one notices or appreciates our service, Jesus does. This knowledge can be both comforting and motivating. On one hand, it means that we are fully known and understood by Jesus. He sees our true selves, including our willingness to serve others selflessly. On the other hand, it reminds us that our servanthood matters to Jesus and that He is always there to recognize and reward our efforts.

Jesus knowing our servanthood means He is aware of every time we serve, whether it is in our community, our church, our school, or even our own homes. Life is full of opportunities to serve, such as volunteering at a local shelter, helping a neighbor with their groceries, tutoring a classmate, or taking care of a family member. Jesus's knowledge of our servanthood assures us that He is always aware of our actions and understands the effort and love behind them. He knows when we go out of our way to help others, even when it is inconvenient or challenging. His awareness of our servanthood can be a great source of comfort and motivation. Knowing that Jesus sees and cares about our efforts can inspire us to continue serving, even when it is difficult.

One of the most comforting aspects of Jesus knowing our servanthood is His recognition and appreciation of it. In Matthew 20:27, Jesus teaches that true greatness comes from serving others. This means that Jesus values our servanthood and acknowledges the love and dedication behind it. His recognition assures us that our efforts do not go unnoticed and that He appreciates every act of kindness and generosity. Jesus's appreciation can bring us great peace and reassurance, knowing that we are making a positive impact and that our servanthood is meaningful and valued.

Jesus's understanding of our servanthood also means that He is aware of the personal sacrifices and efforts involved. He knows that serving others often requires us to give up our time, our resources, our comfort, or our personal desires. Jesus sees the moments when we choose to put others first and the times when we serve from our own need. His awareness of the personal cost of our servanthood assures us that He understands the depth of our commitment and the love that motivates our actions. By recognizing the effort and cost involved, Jesus offers us His support and encouragement to continue serving for the good of others.

Moreover, Jesus's knowledge of our servanthood includes His understanding of the impact it has on others. He sees how our acts of service benefit those around us and contribute to the greater good. Jesus understands that our servanthood can bring hope, comfort, and support to others, and He values the positive impact we make. His understanding helps us to see the bigger picture and to appreciate the importance of our actions. By trusting in Jesus's guidance, we can be confident that our servanthood is making a difference and that it is part of His plan for bringing love and goodness into the world.

Another important aspect of Jesus knowing our servanthood is His understanding of our need for balance and self-care. While serving others is important, it is also essential to take care of ourselves and ensure that we do not become overwhelmed or exhausted. Jesus knows that we need to find a healthy balance between serving others and taking care of our own needs. His guidance can help us to set boundaries, to recognize when we need rest, and to find ways to recharge and renew our strength. By following Jesus's example, we can learn to serve in a sustainable way that allows us to continue giving without burning out.

Understanding that Jesus knows all our servanthood can also deepen our faith and trust in Him. When we recognize that Jesus is aware of every act of service and is always guiding and supporting us, it can strengthen our relationship with Him. This deepened faith can bring us closer to Jesus and help us to rely on His guidance and support in our daily lives. Our relationship with Him can become a source of strength and comfort, providing a solid foundation to stand on in times of difficulty and service. Jesus's knowledge of our servanthood is a testament to His unwavering love and commitment to us, fostering a deeper and more meaningful connection with Him.

Furthermore, Jesus's knowledge of our servanthood includes His understanding of our motivations and intentions. He knows the love and generosity that drive our actions, even when we do not receive recognition or praise from others. Jesus understands that our servanthood is often motivated by a desire to help and to make a positive impact. His understanding assures us that He values the purity and sincerity of our intentions, regardless of the outward acknowledgment we receive. By trusting in Jesus's knowledge of our hearts, we can be confident that our servanthood is seen and appreciated by Him.

Moreover, understanding that Jesus knows our servanthood can inspire us to live with integrity and accountability. Knowing that Jesus sees all our actions and understands our motivations can motivate us to make choices that reflect our faith and values. It can encourage us to be honest, responsible, and ethical in everything we do. Jesus's knowledge of our servanthood is a reminder that we are accountable for our actions and that our choices matter. By living with integrity, we can honor Jesus and build a life that is pleasing to Him.

In conclusion, understanding that the Lord knows all about our servanthood, as described in Matthew 20:27, is a profound and comforting truth. Jesus's complete knowledge of our servanthood means that He sees and understands every act of kindness, every effort to help others, and every moment of dedication. His knowledge includes His recognition and appreciation, His awareness of the personal sacrifices and efforts involved, His understanding of the impact on others, His guidance for balance and self-care, His understanding of our motivations and intentions, and His call for integrity and accountability. This comprehensive understanding of our servanthood can bring us great comfort and motivation, knowing that we are fully known and fully loved by Jesus. It can inspire us to seek His guidance, to trust in His recognition and appreciation, to find balance and self-care, to live with integrity and accountability, and to deepen our faith. Embracing this truth can transform our lives, fostering a deeper relationship with Jesus and a greater sense of peace, hope, and joy in our daily walk with Him. Jesus's knowledge of our servanthood is a testament to His divine wisdom, love, and compassion, offering us the opportunity for growth, fulfillment, and transformation in our journey of faith. This understanding can change our lives, helping us to live in the light of His truth and love, and to become the people He created us to be, strengthened and uplifted by His presence in our servanthood.

Chapter 21 - Your Sincerity

"By this shall all men know that ye are my disciples, if ye have love one to another." (John 13:35)

This verse shows that Jesus, the Son of God, values sincerity and understands the importance of genuine love and kindness towards others. Jesus's knowledge of our sincerity means that He sees every genuine act of love, every moment of kindness, and every effort we make to be truthful and authentic. This deep understanding is part of His divine nature. Knowing our sincerity means that Jesus is fully aware of the honesty in our hearts, the truthfulness of our words, and the authenticity of our actions. Even when we feel like no one notices or appreciates our sincere efforts, Jesus does. This knowledge can be both comforting and motivating. On one hand, it means that we are fully known and understood by Jesus. He sees our true selves, including our genuine intentions and heartfelt actions. On the other hand, it reminds us that our sincerity matters to Jesus and that He is always there to recognize and reward our efforts.

Jesus knowing our sincerity means He is aware of every time we act out of genuine love and kindness, whether it is in our community, our church, our school, or even our own homes. Life is full of opportunities to show sincerity, such as helping a friend in need, speaking truthfully even when it is difficult, offering a kind word to someone who is hurting, or standing up for what is right. Jesus's knowledge of our sincerity assures us that He is always aware of our actions and understands the honesty and love behind them. He knows when we go out of our way to be kind and truthful, even when it is inconvenient or challenging. His awareness of our sincerity can be a great source of comfort and motivation. Knowing that Jesus sees and cares about our genuine efforts can inspire us to continue being sincere, even when it is difficult.

One of the most comforting aspects of Jesus knowing our sincerity is His recognition and appreciation of it. In John 13:35, Jesus teaches that our love for one another is the hallmark of being His disciples. This means that Jesus values our sincerity and acknowledges the love and authenticity behind it. His recognition assures us that our efforts to be genuine do not go unnoticed and that He appreciates every act of kindness and honesty. Jesus's appreciation can bring us great peace and reassurance, knowing that we are making a positive impact and that our sincerity is meaningful and valued.

Jesus's understanding of our sincerity also means that He is aware of the personal challenges and struggles involved. He knows that being sincere often requires us to go against our natural inclinations, to make difficult choices, and to endure hardships. Jesus sees the moments when we choose to act with integrity and honesty, even when it is difficult or uncomfortable. His awareness of the personal cost of our sincerity assures us that He understands the depth of our commitment and the love that motivates our actions. By recognizing the effort and sacrifices involved, Jesus offers us His support and encouragement to continue being sincere for the good of others.

Moreover, Jesus's knowledge of our sincerity includes His understanding of the positive impact it has on others. He sees how our genuine acts of love and kindness benefit those around us and contribute to the greater good. Jesus understands that our sincerity can bring hope, comfort, and support to others, and He values the positive impact we make. His understanding helps us to see the bigger picture and to appreciate the importance of our actions. By trusting in Jesus's guidance, we can be confident that our sincerity is making a difference and that it is part of His plan for bringing love and goodness into the world.

Another important aspect of Jesus knowing our sincerity is His understanding of our need for strength and perseverance. While being sincere is important, it is also essential to have the strength and perseverance to continue being genuine, even in the face of adversity. Jesus knows that we need His strength to remain faithful and to overcome the challenges we face. His guidance can help us to find the strength and determination to continue being sincere, even when it is difficult. By following Jesus's example, we can learn to rely on His strength and to trust in His guidance as we navigate the challenges of life.

Understanding that Jesus knows all our sincerity can also deepen our faith and trust in Him. When we recognize that Jesus is aware of every genuine act of love and kindness and is always guiding and supporting us, it can strengthen our relationship with Him. This deepened faith can bring us closer to Jesus and help us to rely on His guidance and support in our daily lives. Our relationship with Him can become a source of strength and comfort, providing a solid foundation to stand on in times of difficulty and challenge. Jesus's knowledge of our sincerity is a testament to His unwavering love and commitment to us, fostering a deeper and more meaningful connection with Him.

Furthermore, Jesus's knowledge of our sincerity includes His understanding of our motivations and intentions. He knows the love and authenticity that drive our actions, even when we do not receive recognition or praise from others. Jesus understands that our sincerity is often motivated by a desire to honor Him and to live according to His will. His understanding assures us that He values the purity and sincerity of our intentions, regardless of the outward acknowledgment we receive. By trusting in Jesus's knowledge of our hearts, we can be confident that our sincerity is seen and appreciated by Him.

Moreover, understanding that Jesus knows our sincerity can inspire us to live with integrity and accountability. Knowing that Jesus sees all our actions and understands our motivations can motivate us to make choices that reflect our faith and values. It can encourage us to be honest, responsible, and ethical in everything we do. Jesus's knowledge of our sincerity is a reminder that we are accountable for our actions and that our choices matter. By living with integrity, we can honor Jesus and build a life that is pleasing to Him.

In conclusion, understanding that the Lord knows all about our sincerity, as described in John 13:35, is a profound and comforting truth. Jesus's complete knowledge of our sincerity means that He sees and understands every genuine act of love, every moment of kindness, and every effort to be truthful and authentic. His knowledge includes His recognition and appreciation, His awareness of the personal challenges and struggles involved, His understanding of the positive impact of our sincerity, His guidance for strength and perseverance, His understanding of our motivations and intentions, and His call for integrity and accountability. This comprehensive understanding of our sincerity can bring us great comfort and motivation, knowing that we are fully known and fully loved by Jesus. It can inspire us to seek His guidance, to trust in His recognition and appreciation, to find strength and perseverance, to live with integrity and accountability, and to deepen our faith. Embracing this truth can transform our lives, fostering a deeper relationship with Jesus and a greater sense of peace, hope, and joy in our daily walk with Him. Jesus's knowledge of our sincerity is a testament to His divine wisdom, love, and compassion, offering us the opportunity for growth, fulfillment, and transformation in our journey of faith. This understanding can change our lives, helping us to live in the light of His truth and love, and to become the people He created us to be, strengthened and uplifted by His presence in our sincerity.

Chapter 22 - Your Sorrows

"I say unto you, that likewise joy shall be in heaven over one sinner that repenteth..." (Luke 15:7)

This verse shows that Jesus, the Son of God, is deeply aware of our sorrows, especially those connected to our struggles, mistakes, and the heavy burden of sin. Jesus's knowledge of our sorrows means that He sees every tear we shed, every heartache we endure, and every moment of pain we experience. This deep understanding is part of His divine nature. Knowing our sorrows means that Jesus is fully aware of our emotional, physical, and spiritual suffering. Even when we feel like no one understands the depth of our sorrow, Jesus does. This knowledge can be both comforting and motivating. On one hand, it means that we are fully known and understood by Jesus. He sees our true selves, including our deepest pains and regrets. On the other hand, it reminds us that our sorrows matter to Jesus and that He is always there to provide comfort, strength, and hope.

Jesus knowing our sorrows means He is aware of every trial and tribulation we face, especially when we suffer because of our own mistakes or sins. Life is filled with moments that can bring sorrow, such as losing a loved one, facing rejection, dealing with illness, or experiencing failure. Jesus's knowledge of our sorrows assures us that He is always aware of our struggles and understands the pain we go through. He knows the weight of our guilt, the sting of our regrets, and the heaviness of our grief. His awareness of our sorrows can be a great source of comfort and motivation. Knowing that Jesus sees and cares about our pain can inspire us to turn to Him for support and to trust that He is with us every step of the way.

One of the most comforting aspects of Jesus knowing our sorrows is His promise of joy and redemption. In Luke 15:7, Jesus speaks of the joy in heaven over one sinner who repents. This promise means that Jesus offers us a path to healing and joy, even in the midst of our deepest sorrows. His promise assures us that our sorrow is not the end of the story and that there is hope for a brighter future. Jesus's promise of joy and redemption can bring us great reassurance and hope, knowing that we are not alone in our struggles and that He is working for our good.

Jesus's understanding of our sorrows also means that He is aware of the strength and resilience it takes to endure pain and hardship. Life's challenges can test our faith and perseverance, but Jesus sees our efforts to remain strong and to keep moving forward. He understands the courage it takes to face each day with hope and determination, even when the weight of sorrow feels overwhelming. His presence in our lives can provide us with the strength and encouragement we need to persevere. By relying on Jesus's strength, we can find the resilience to endure our sorrows and to emerge stronger on the other side.

Moreover, Jesus's knowledge of our sorrows includes His awareness of our need for comfort and healing. He knows that sorrow can leave deep wounds in our hearts and souls. Jesus offers us His healing touch, bringing comfort and restoration to our brokenness. His compassion assures us that He is with us in our pain, offering His love and support. Jesus's healing is not just about removing the pain but also about helping us to grow and find new strength in the midst of our sorrow. His understanding and compassion can bring us comfort, knowing that we are not alone in our pain and that He is always working to bring healing and wholeness to our lives.

Another important aspect of Jesus knowing our sorrows is His understanding of the different ways we cope with pain. Everyone deals with sorrow differently, and Jesus sees and understands our individual coping mechanisms. Whether we seek comfort in prayer, turn to friends and family, or find solace in nature or hobbies, Jesus knows what we need to heal and cope. His understanding helps us to find healthy and constructive ways to deal with our pain. He guides us towards activities and practices that can bring us peace and healing. By following His guidance, we can navigate our sorrows in a way that leads to growth and renewal.

Understanding that Jesus knows all our sorrows can also deepen our faith and trust in Him. When we recognize that Jesus is aware of every aspect of our pain and is always guiding and supporting us, it can strengthen our relationship with Him. This deepened faith can bring us closer to Jesus and help us to rely on His guidance and support. Our relationship with Him can become a source of strength and comfort, providing a solid foundation to stand on in times of trouble. Jesus's knowledge of our sorrows is a testament to His unwavering love and commitment to us, fostering a deeper and more meaningful connection with Him.

Furthermore, Jesus's knowledge of our sorrows includes His understanding of our need for purpose and meaning in the midst of pain. He knows that we all have a desire to understand why we suffer and to find meaning in our experiences. Jesus provides us with opportunities to find purpose in our sorrow by guiding us towards ways to use our pain for good. He knows our strengths and weaknesses and helps us to use them in ways that bring healing and hope to others. His guidance ensures that our sorrow is not in vain but can be transformed into a source of strength and inspiration for ourselves and others.

Moreover, understanding that Jesus knows our sorrows can inspire us to live with compassion and empathy towards others. Knowing that Jesus sees and understands our pain can motivate us to reach out to those who are suffering and offer our support and love. Jesus's example of compassion teaches us to be there for others in their times of need, to listen to their pain, and to offer a comforting presence. By following His example, we can create a community of support and encouragement, helping each other to navigate the challenges of life.

In conclusion, understanding that the Lord knows all about our sorrows, as described in Luke 15:7, is a profound and comforting truth. Jesus's complete knowledge of our sorrows means that He sees and understands every tear we shed, every heartache we endure, and every moment of pain we experience. His knowledge includes His promise of joy and redemption, His support in our strength and resilience, His awareness of our need for comfort and healing, His guidance in coping with pain, His understanding of our need for purpose and meaning, and His call for compassion and empathy towards others. This comprehensive understanding of our sorrows can bring us great comfort and motivation, knowing that we are fully known and fully loved by Jesus. It can inspire us to seek His guidance, to trust in His promise of joy and redemption, to find strength and resilience in His presence, to seek comfort and healing in His love, to find purpose and meaning in our pain, to live with compassion and empathy, and to deepen our faith. Embracing this truth can transform our lives, fostering a deeper relationship with Jesus and a greater sense of peace, hope, and joy in our daily walk with Him. Jesus's knowledge of our sorrows is a testament to His divine wisdom, love, and compassion, offering us the opportunity for growth, fulfillment, and transformation in our experiences of pain and hardship. This understanding can change our lives, helping us to live in the light of His truth and love, and to become the people He created us to be, strengthened and healed by His presence in our sorrows.

Chapter 23 - Your Self-Denial

"And he said to them all, If any man will come after me, let him deny himself, and take up his cross daily, and follow me." (Luke 9:23) This verse shows that Jesus, the Son of God, values our self-denial and understands the challenges we face when we choose to put aside our own desires to follow Him. Jesus's knowledge of our self-denial means that He sees every sacrifice we make, every moment of self-control, and every effort to prioritize His will over our own. This deep understanding is part of His divine nature. Knowing our self-denial means that Jesus is fully aware of the ways we strive to live according to His teachings, even when it requires us to give up something important to us. Even when we feel like no one notices or appreciates our sacrifices, Jesus does. This knowledge can be both comforting and motivating. On one hand, it means that we are fully known and understood by Jesus. He sees our true selves, including our willingness to deny ourselves for His sake. On the other hand, it reminds us that our self-denial matters to Jesus and that He is always there to provide strength and encouragement.

Jesus knowing our self-denial means He is aware of every time we choose to follow His path instead of our own, whether it is in our decisions, our actions, or our thoughts. Life is full of opportunities to practice self-denial, such as choosing to forgive someone who has hurt us, deciding to act with kindness instead of anger, spending time in prayer and Bible study instead of engaging in leisure activities, or making financial sacrifices to help those in need. Jesus's knowledge of our self-denial assures us that He is always aware of our actions and understands the effort and love behind them. He knows when we resist temptation, when we choose integrity over dishonesty, and when we put others' needs before our own. His awareness of our self-denial can be a great source of comfort and motivation. Knowing that Jesus sees and cares about our efforts can inspire us to continue practicing self-denial, even when it is challenging.

One of the most comforting aspects of Jesus knowing our self-denial is His recognition and appreciation of it. In Luke 9:23, Jesus calls us to deny ourselves, take up our cross daily, and follow Him. This means that Jesus values our self-denial and acknowledges the love and dedication behind it. His recognition assures us that our efforts to deny ourselves do not go unnoticed and that He appreciates every act of self-control and sacrifice. Jesus's appreciation can bring us great peace and reassurance, knowing that we are making a positive impact and that our self-denial is meaningful and valued.

Jesus's understanding of our self-denial also means that He is aware of the personal challenges and struggles involved. He knows that denying ourselves often requires us to go against our natural inclinations, to make difficult choices, and to endure hardships. Jesus sees the moments when we choose to follow His will, even when it is difficult or uncomfortable. His awareness of the personal cost of our self-denial assures us that He understands the depth of our commitment and the love that motivates our actions. By recognizing the effort and sacrifices involved, Jesus offers us His support and encouragement to continue practicing self-denial for the good of others.

Moreover, Jesus's knowledge of our self-denial includes His understanding of the positive impact it has on our lives and the lives of others. He sees how our acts of self-denial benefit those around us and contribute to the greater good. Jesus understands that our self-denial can lead to greater peace, joy, and fulfillment in our own lives, as well as in the lives of those we serve and influence. His understanding helps us to see the bigger picture and to appreciate the importance of our actions. By trusting in Jesus's guidance, we can be confident that our self-denial is making a difference and that it is part of His plan for bringing love and goodness into the world.

Another important aspect of Jesus knowing our self-denial is His understanding of our need for balance and self-care. While denying ourselves is important, it is also essential to take care of ourselves and ensure that we do not become overwhelmed or exhausted. Jesus knows that we need to find a healthy balance between self-denial and taking care of our own needs. His guidance can help us to set boundaries, to recognize when we need rest, and to find ways to recharge and renew our strength. By following Jesus's example, we can learn to practice self-denial in a sustainable way that allows us to continue giving without burning out.

Understanding that Jesus knows all our self-denial can also deepen our faith and trust in Him. When we recognize that Jesus is aware of every act of self-control and sacrifice and is always guiding and supporting us, it can strengthen our relationship with Him. This deepened faith can bring us closer to Jesus and help us to rely on His guidance and support in our daily lives. Our relationship with Him can become a source of strength and comfort, providing a solid foundation to stand on in times of difficulty and challenge. Jesus's knowledge of our self-denial is a testament to His unwavering love and commitment to us, fostering a deeper and more meaningful connection with Him.

Furthermore, Jesus's knowledge of our self-denial includes His understanding of our motivations and intentions. He knows the love and dedication that drive our actions, even when we do not receive recognition or praise from others. Jesus understands that our self-denial is often motivated by a desire to honor Him and to live according to His will. His understanding assures us that He values the purity and sincerity of our intentions, regardless of the outward acknowledgment we receive. By trusting in Jesus's knowledge of our hearts, we can be confident that our self-denial is seen and appreciated by Him.

Moreover, understanding that Jesus knows our self-denial can inspire us to live with integrity and accountability. Knowing that Jesus sees all our actions and understands our motivations can motivate us to make choices that reflect our faith and values. It can encourage us to be honest, responsible, and ethical in everything we do. Jesus's knowledge of our self-denial is a reminder that we are accountable for our actions and that our choices matter. By living with integrity, we can honor Jesus and build a life that is pleasing to Him.

In conclusion, understanding that the Lord knows all about our self-denial, as described in Luke 9:23, is a profound and comforting truth. Jesus's complete knowledge of our self-denial means that He sees and understands every sacrifice we make, every moment of self-control, and every effort to prioritize His will over our own. His knowledge includes His recognition and appreciation, His awareness of the personal challenges and struggles involved, His understanding of the positive impact of our self-denial, His guidance for balance and self-care, His understanding of our motivations and intentions, and His call for integrity and accountability. This comprehensive understanding of our self-denial can bring us great comfort and motivation, knowing that we are fully known and fully loved by Jesus. It can inspire us to seek His guidance, to trust in His recognition and appreciation, to find balance and self-care, to live with integrity and accountability, and to deepen our faith. Embracing this truth can transform our lives, fostering a deeper relationship with Jesus and a greater sense of peace, hope, and joy in our daily walk with Him. Jesus's knowledge of our self-denial is a testament to His divine wisdom, love, and compassion, offering us the opportunity for growth, fulfillment, and transformation in our journey of faith. This understanding can change our lives, helping us to live in the light of His truth and love, and to become the people He created us to be, strengthened and uplifted by His presence in our self-denial.

Chapter 24 - Your Sacrificial Love

"Greater love hath no man than this, that a man lay down his life for his friends." (John 15:13)

This verse shows that Jesus, the Son of God, values our sacrificial love and understands the depth of love that leads us to make sacrifices for others. Jesus's knowledge of our sacrificial love means that He sees every act of selflessness, every moment of putting others first, and every time we choose to give up something for the sake of someone else. This deep understanding is part of His divine nature. Knowing our sacrificial love means that Jesus is fully aware of the ways we show love through our actions, even when it requires significant personal cost. Even when we feel like no one notices or appreciates our sacrifices, Jesus does. This knowledge can be both comforting and motivating. On one hand, it means that we are fully known and understood by Jesus. He sees our true selves, including our willingness to make sacrifices out of love for others. On the other hand, it reminds us that our sacrificial love matters to Jesus and that He is always there to recognize and reward our efforts.

Jesus knowing our sacrificial love means He is aware of every time we choose to put others' needs before our own, whether it is in our family, our friendships, our community, or even for strangers. Life is full of opportunities to demonstrate sacrificial love, such as caring for a sick family member, staying up late to comfort a friend in distress, volunteering time to help those in need, or even making financial sacrifices to support someone struggling. Jesus's knowledge of our sacrificial love assures us that He is always aware of our actions and understands the effort and love behind them. He knows when we go out of our way to help others, even when it is inconvenient or challenging. His awareness of our sacrificial love can be a great source of comfort and motivation. Knowing that Jesus sees and cares about our efforts can inspire us to continue showing love, even when it is difficult.

One of the most comforting aspects of Jesus knowing our sacrificial love is His recognition and appreciation of it. In John 15:13, Jesus teaches that the greatest love is shown when someone lays down their life for their friends. This means that Jesus values our sacrificial love and acknowledges the depth of love and dedication behind it. His recognition assures us that our efforts to love sacrificially do not go unnoticed and that He appreciates every act of selflessness and generosity. Jesus's appreciation can bring us great peace and reassurance, knowing that we are making a positive impact and that our sacrificial love is meaningful and valued.

Jesus's understanding of our sacrificial love also means that He is aware of the personal challenges and struggles involved. He knows that loving sacrificially often requires us to give up our time, our resources, our comfort, or our personal desires. Jesus sees the moments when we choose to put others first and the times when we give from our own need. His awareness of the personal cost of our sacrificial love assures us that He understands the depth of our commitment and the love that motivates our actions. By recognizing the effort and sacrifices involved, Jesus offers us His support and encouragement to continue showing sacrificial love for the good of others.

Moreover, Jesus's knowledge of our sacrificial love includes His understanding of the positive impact it has on others. He sees how our acts of sacrificial love benefit those around us and contribute to the greater good. Jesus understands that our sacrificial love can bring hope, comfort, and support to others, and He values the positive impact we make. His understanding helps us to see the bigger picture and to appreciate the importance of our actions. By trusting in Jesus's guidance, we can be confident that our sacrificial love is making a difference and that it is part of His plan for bringing love and goodness into the world.

Another important aspect of Jesus knowing our sacrificial love is His understanding of our need for balance and self-care. While showing sacrificial love is important, it is also essential to take care of ourselves and to ensure that we do not become overwhelmed or exhausted. Jesus knows that we need to find a healthy balance between giving to others and taking care of our own needs. His guidance can help us to set boundaries, to recognize when we need rest, and to find ways to recharge and renew our strength. By following Jesus's example, we can learn to show sacrificial love in a sustainable way that allows us to continue giving without burning out.

Understanding that Jesus knows all our sacrificial love can also deepen our faith and trust in Him. When we recognize that Jesus is aware of every act of selflessness and sacrifice and is always guiding and supporting us, it can strengthen our relationship with Him. This deepened faith can bring us closer to Jesus and help us to rely on His guidance and support in our daily lives. Our relationship with Him can become a source of strength and comfort, providing a solid foundation to stand on in times of difficulty and challenge. Jesus's knowledge of our sacrificial love is a testament to His unwavering love and commitment to us, fostering a deeper and more meaningful connection with Him.

Furthermore, Jesus's knowledge of our sacrificial love includes His understanding of our motivations and intentions. He knows the love and dedication that drive our actions, even when we do not receive recognition or praise from others. Jesus understands that our sacrificial love is often motivated by a desire to honor Him and to live according to His will. His understanding assures us that He values the purity and sincerity of our intentions, regardless of the outward acknowledgment we receive. By trusting in Jesus's knowledge of our hearts, we can be confident that our sacrificial love is seen and appreciated by Him.

Moreover, understanding that Jesus knows our sacrificial love can inspire us to live with integrity and accountability. Knowing that Jesus sees all our actions and understands our motivations can motivate us to make choices that reflect our faith and values. It can encourage us to be honest, responsible, and ethical in everything we do. Jesus's knowledge of our sacrificial love is a reminder that we are accountable for our actions and that our choices matter. By living with integrity, we can honor Jesus and build a life that is pleasing to Him.

In conclusion, understanding that the Lord knows all about our sacrificial love, as described in John 15:13, is a profound and comforting truth. Jesus's complete knowledge of our sacrificial love means that He sees and understands every act of selflessness, every moment of putting others first, and every time we choose to give up something for the sake of someone else. His knowledge includes His recognition and appreciation, His awareness of the personal challenges and struggles involved, His understanding of the positive impact of our sacrificial love, His guidance for balance and self-care, His understanding of our motivations and intentions, and His call for integrity and accountability. This comprehensive understanding of our sacrificial love can bring us great comfort and motivation, knowing that we are fully known and fully loved by Jesus. It can inspire us to seek His guidance, to trust in His recognition and appreciation, to find balance and self-care, to live with integrity and accountability, and to deepen our faith. Embracing this truth can transform our lives, fostering a deeper relationship with Jesus and a greater sense of peace, hope, and joy in our daily walk with Him. Jesus's knowledge of our sacrificial love is a testament to His divine wisdom, love, and compassion, offering us the opportunity for growth, fulfillment, and transformation in our journey of faith. This understanding can change our lives, helping us to live in the light of His truth and love, and to become the people He created us to be, strengthened and uplifted by His presence in our sacrificial love.

Chapter 25 - Your Spiritual Worship

"But the hour cometh, and now is, when the true worshippers shall worship the Father in spirit and in truth..." (John 4:23)

This verse shows that Jesus, the Son of God, values our spiritual worship and understands the depth and sincerity behind our acts of worship. Jesus's knowledge of our spiritual worship means that He sees every prayer we whisper, every song of praise we sing, and every moment we spend in silent adoration. This deep understanding is part of His divine nature. Knowing our spiritual worship means that Jesus is fully aware of the ways we strive to connect with God, to honor Him, and to express our love and reverence for Him. Even when we feel like our acts of worship go unnoticed or unappreciated by others, Jesus does notice. This knowledge can be both comforting and motivating. On one hand, it means that we are fully known and understood by Jesus. He sees our true selves, including our heartfelt worship and devotion. On the other hand, it reminds us that our spiritual worship matters to Jesus and that He is always there to receive and acknowledge our acts of worship.

Jesus knowing our spiritual worship means He is aware of every time we choose to connect with God, whether it is through prayer, singing, reading the Bible, or simply being still in His presence. Life is full of opportunities to worship God in spirit and in truth, such as attending church services, participating in prayer groups, spending time in personal devotion, or expressing gratitude for His blessings. Jesus's knowledge of our spiritual worship assures us that He is always aware of our actions and understands the sincerity and love behind them. He knows when we seek to draw closer to God, when we express our faith through worship, and when we strive to live according to His teachings. His awareness of our spiritual worship can be a great source of comfort and motivation. Knowing that Jesus sees and values our worship can inspire us to continue seeking Him, even when it is difficult.

One of the most comforting aspects of Jesus knowing our spiritual worship is His recognition and appreciation of it. In John 4:23, Jesus teaches that true worshippers shall worship the Father in spirit and in truth. This means that Jesus values our spiritual worship and acknowledges the depth of devotion and sincerity behind it. His recognition assures us that our efforts to worship do not go unnoticed and that He appreciates every act of devotion and praise. Jesus's appreciation can bring us great peace and reassurance, knowing that our worship is meaningful and valued.

Jesus's understanding of our spiritual worship also means that He is aware of the personal challenges and struggles involved. He knows that worshipping in spirit and in truth often requires us to go beyond routine and ritual, to connect with God on a deeper, more personal level, and to be genuine in our expressions of faith. Jesus sees the moments when we choose to worship sincerely, even when it is difficult or uncomfortable. His awareness of the personal cost of our spiritual worship assures us that He understands the depth of our commitment and the love that motivates our actions. By recognizing the effort and sincerity involved, Jesus offers us His support and encouragement to continue worshipping in spirit and in truth.

Moreover, Jesus's knowledge of our spiritual worship includes His understanding of the positive impact it has on our lives and the lives of others. He sees how our acts of worship strengthen our faith, bring us closer to God, and inspire those around us. Jesus understands that our spiritual worship can lead to greater peace, joy, and fulfillment in our own lives, as well as in the lives of those we influence. His understanding helps us to see the bigger picture and to appreciate the importance of our actions. By trusting in Jesus's guidance, we can be confident that our spiritual worship is making a difference and that it is part of His plan for bringing love and goodness into the world.

Another important aspect of Jesus knowing our spiritual worship is His understanding of our need for balance and self-care. While worshipping God is important, it is also essential to take care of ourselves and ensure that we do not become overwhelmed or exhausted. Jesus knows that we need to find a healthy balance between worship and taking care of our own needs. His guidance can help us to set boundaries, to recognize when we need rest, and to find ways to recharge and renew our strength. By following Jesus's example, we can learn to worship in a sustainable way that allows us to continue connecting with God without burning out.

Understanding that Jesus knows all our spiritual worship can also deepen our faith and trust in Him. When we recognize that Jesus is aware of every act of worship and devotion and is always guiding and supporting us, it can strengthen our relationship with Him. This deepened faith can bring us closer to Jesus and help us to rely on His guidance and support in our daily lives. Our relationship with Him can become a source of strength and comfort, providing a solid foundation to stand on in times of difficulty and challenge. Jesus's knowledge of our spiritual worship is a testament to His unwavering love and commitment to us, fostering a deeper and more meaningful connection with Him.

Furthermore, Jesus's knowledge of our spiritual worship includes His understanding of our motivations and intentions. He knows the love and devotion that drive our actions, even when we do not receive recognition or praise from others. Jesus understands that our spiritual worship is often motivated by a desire to honor Him and to live according to His will. His understanding assures us that He values the purity and sincerity of our intentions, regardless of the outward acknowledgment we receive. By trusting in Jesus's knowledge of our hearts, we can be confident that our spiritual worship is seen and appreciated by Him.

Moreover, understanding that Jesus knows our spiritual worship can inspire us to live with integrity and accountability. Knowing that Jesus sees all our actions and understands our motivations can motivate us to make choices that reflect our faith and values. It can encourage us to be honest, responsible, and ethical in everything we do. Jesus's knowledge of our spiritual worship is a reminder that we are accountable for our actions and that our choices matter. By living with integrity, we can honor Jesus and build a life that is pleasing to Him.

In conclusion, understanding that the Lord knows all about our spiritual worship, as described in John 4:23, is a profound and comforting truth. Jesus's complete knowledge of our spiritual worship means that He sees and understands every prayer we whisper, every song of praise we sing, and every moment we spend in silent adoration. His knowledge includes His recognition and appreciation, His awareness of the personal challenges and struggles involved, His understanding of the positive impact of our spiritual worship, His guidance for balance and self-care, His understanding of our motivations and intentions, and His call for integrity and accountability. This comprehensive understanding of our spiritual worship can bring us great comfort and motivation, knowing that we are fully known and fully loved by Jesus. It can inspire us to seek His guidance, to trust in His recognition and appreciation, to find balance and self-care, to live with integrity and accountability, and to deepen our faith. Embracing this truth can transform our lives, fostering a deeper relationship with Jesus and a greater sense of peace, hope, and joy in our daily walk with Him. Jesus's knowledge of our spiritual worship is a testament to His divine wisdom, love, and compassion, offering us the opportunity for growth, fulfillment, and transformation in our journey of faith. This understanding can change our lives, helping us to live in the light of His truth and love, and to become the people He created us to be, strengthened and uplifted by His presence in our spiritual worship.

Conclusion

As we conclude "Jesus Knows: Our Hearts, Our Responsibility," it is clear that the journey of understanding how intimately Jesus knows us is both deeply humbling and profoundly empowering. The truth that Jesus sees into the depths of our hearts—our thoughts, desires, struggles, and motivations—places a significant responsibility on each of us. This knowledge should not be taken lightly, for it calls us to a life of greater integrity, authenticity, and commitment to God's will.

Throughout this book, we have explored how Jesus' perfect knowledge of our hearts impacts every aspect of our lives. He sees beyond our outward actions to the true intentions that drive us. This divine insight challenges us to live with a higher standard of righteousness, one that goes beyond mere appearances and touches the core of who we are. It is not enough to perform good deeds or to say the right words; we are called to align our hearts with God's truth, to let our innermost thoughts and desires reflect His love and holiness.

Yet, with this responsibility comes an incredible comfort. Knowing that Jesus understands us completely means that He sees our efforts, our struggles, and our sincere desire to follow Him, even when we fall short. He knows the fears we wrestle with, the pain we carry, and the burdens we bear. And in His perfect understanding, He offers us grace, forgiveness, and strength to continue growing in faith. Jesus' knowledge of our hearts is not just about judgment; it is also about compassion and a deep, abiding love that seeks to guide us closer to Him.

The responsibility that comes with being known by Jesus should inspire us to cultivate a heart that is fully devoted to God. It challenges us to regularly examine our motives, to confess when we have gone astray, and to seek the Holy Spirit's guidance in transforming our inner lives. This ongoing process of self-examination and spiritual growth is vital, for it shapes the very essence of who we are and how we live out our faith in the world.

As you reflect on the insights shared in this book, I encourage you to embrace the dual reality of being fully known and fully loved by Jesus. Let this truth motivate you to live with greater integrity, to pursue righteousness with sincerity, and to rely on God's grace in every area of your life. The responsibility that comes with Jesus' knowledge of our hearts is not a burden to be feared but a privilege to be embraced. It is an opportunity to grow closer to God, to become more like Christ, and to live a life that honors the One who knows us best.

In the end, "Jesus Knows: Our Hearts, Our Responsibility" is a call to action. It is a reminder that while we cannot hide from God, we also do not need to. Instead, we are invited to open our hearts to Him, to allow His love and truth to transform us, and to live each day with the knowledge that we are fully known, fully loved, and fully empowered to fulfill the purposes He has for our lives. May this truth guide you, strengthen you, and lead you to a deeper, more authentic relationship with Jesus Christ.

Don't miss out!

Visit the website below and you can sign up to receive emails whenever Joshua Rhoades publishes a new book. There's no charge and no obligation.

https://books2read.com/r/B-A-AJLBB-WGBYE

BOOKS 2 READ

Connecting independent readers to independent writers.

Did you love *Jesus Knows- Our Hearts, Our Responsibility*? Then you should read *Renewed Hope- How to Find Encouragement in God*[1] by Joshua Rhoades!

[2]

In a world where challenges and hardships seem to come at us from every side, it's easy to feel overwhelmed, discouraged, and even hopeless. We all face moments when we wonder how we will ever make it through the difficulties we encounter. But in these times, the Bible offers us a powerful example of finding strength and hope, no matter the circumstances. In 1 Samuel 30:6, we read about David, a man who faced great trials and overwhelming odds, yet in the midst of it all, "David encouraged himself in the LORD his God." This simple yet profound statement serves as the foundation for this book, "Renewed Hope- How to Find Encouragement in God." David's life was filled with ups and downs, moments of triumph and times of deep despair. He knew what it was like to be pursued by enemies, to experience loss, and to feel abandoned. Yet, even in his darkest hours, David found a way to renew his hope by turning to God. He didn't rely on his own strength or seek comfort in worldly solutions. Instead, he looked to the LORD, drawing strength and encouragement from his relationship

---

1. https://books2read.com/u/boeko1

2. https://books2read.com/u/boeko1

with God. This book is an invitation to explore how we, too, can find renewed hope and encouragement in God, just as David did. It is a guide to understanding the power of faith, prayer, and trusting in God's promises, even when life seems unbearable. Throughout these pages, we will explore practical ways to draw closer to God, to encourage ourselves in Him, and to discover the peace and strength that come from relying on the LORD. Whether you are facing a specific challenge right now or simply want to deepen your relationship with God, this book will provide you with the tools and inspiration you need to find encouragement in the LORD. As we journey together through the principles found in David's example, you will learn how to shift your focus from the problems that surround you to the God who sustains you. You will discover that no matter what life throws at you, there is always hope in the LORD, and by encouraging yourself in Him, you can face any situation with renewed strength and confidence. This is not just a book about surviving difficult times, but about thriving through them by finding your hope and encouragement in the unchanging character of God. So, whether you are struggling with personal challenges, feeling weighed down by the burdens of life, or simply seeking a deeper sense of peace and purpose, "Renewed Hope-How to Find Encouragement in God" is here to remind you that you are not alone, and that with God, there is always a reason to hope. Let David's example inspire you to turn to the LORD, to find your strength in Him, and to walk forward with a renewed sense of hope, no matter what you face.